Library of Congress Cataloging-in-Publication Data has
been applied for.

ISBN-13: 978-0-578-86533-1

Visit www.heavenlyflood.com

First edition 2021

HEAVENLY
FLOOD

The Fascinating *Astrological* Origins of

Noah's Ark and the Great Flood

S.H. Scholar

Preface

Ever since the decipherment of cuneiform and the subsequent translations of newly discovered ancient texts, academics have accepted that the biblical flood story originated from many older proto-flood tales from the Near East. The unsettling consequence is that our beliefs about the cultural influences that helped form the foundation of Western civilization needs to be reassessed. This profound and humbling realization has much wider implications than simply adding to our knowledge of the past for it challenges the very origins of Western identity. However, despite this, or perhaps because of it, this new direction has failed to generate the type of interest in the academic community that it deserves, nor has it excited in the public imagination the enthusiasm to explore this aspect of the ancient past.

My own interest in the ancient Near East started many decades ago when I was a child. It happened one rainy afternoon during a visit to the British Museum. For the first time, I was confronted with the reality of an ancient world whose only trace was the objects they left behind. However, there was something about the sterile and academic context in which these objects now found themselves that veiled a deeper reality. Realizing early on that these objects were products of once living minds with their own vastly different interpretation of reality, I quickly became seduced by the idea that if one could reconnect with these earlier cultures without the bias (so far as it is possible) of modern judgment, then one might better be able to place our own modern culture within a wider context.

During the subsequent decades, I spent many thousands of hours researching and translating ancient texts. It is my hope that by sharing some of the insights I gained during this period that the beginnings of the cultural exchange and evolution that eventually formed the foundations for Western civilization will finally be "laid bare."

Chicago 2021
SHS

Contents

Part Three – Celestial Mechanics

Part Four – Heavenly Flood

Appendices

Noah released a dove by Gustave Doré. 1866.

INTRODUCTION

Known by billions of people around the world, the story of Noah's Ark and the Great Flood has inspired and delighted the human imagination ever since it was first recorded over 2,500 years ago. As part of a literary tradition embedded in Western culture, the tale of the flood has had a profound impact on the Western psyche as evidenced by countless artists throughout history who have attempted to recapture the tale. From Michelangelo's sublime ceiling of the Sistine Chapel, all the way up to 21st century blockbuster movies, depictions of the event have remained as popular and influential as ever.

Taken as literal truth by most people throughout history, the tale of the Great Flood has encouraged many to attempt to prove its authenticity. From at least 300 CE through to present day, there has been much speculation and many expeditions to find the remains of Noah's Ark, all of which have failed. Others have tried to confirm the truth of the story by looking for geological evidence of a Great Flood that engulfed the world, again without success.

However, there have been scholars and historians who took a different path, and rather than seek to prove the historicity of the tale, have instead searched for insight by asking, "What was the idea that inspired the narration of the story?" Although this has been a more illuminating approach, it has stopped short of fully explaining the origins and unexplainable endurance of the tale—until now. We are, at last, in a position to provide an answer to that most enigmatic question. Fascinating new research and insight now sheds light on the processes that triggered the development of the Great Flood tale starting with an astronomical event witnessed around 4800 BCE in what is today southern Iraq. The influence of this event was to extend across Mesopotamia for the next several millennia, inspiring numerous versions of the tale which appeared in its wake.

I now invite you to join me in the following pages as we rediscover that remarkable event and explore the profound effect it had on the region and on Abrahamic religions.

A Few Notes About This Book

Most books about the ancient Near East tend to be written in an academic or scholarly manner making them inaccessible to the average reader. This book is different in that it is specifically written for the layperson with little knowledge of the ancient past. Care has been taken to present information and ideas in a simple and concise manner while eliminating anything that might serve as a distraction. However, there may be concepts and terms that the reader may be unfamiliar with and these are presented in ***bold*** and included in a brief glossary.

As part of our examination into the development of the Great Flood tale, this book explores how the narrative evolved over time and, for clarity, the story's development is presented in a linear fashion. However, the reader should note that many versions of the Great Flood tale were celebrated at the same time with older narratives still being copied down by scribes and circulated while newer narratives were being written. This does not cause a problem so long as the reader bears in mind that what is important is *when* a particular narrative first emerged and not when any subsequent copies were produced.

Finally, a note about the terms *astronomy* and *astrology*. In the ancient world, to make astronomical observations was to practice astrology, and to practice astrology was to make astronomical observations. However, there is no modern word in English that captures this idea adequately, and in this text we are forced to use the modern terms *astronomy* and *astrology*. When encountering these terms, you should be aware that their modern meaning should be understood through the lens of the ancient mind for who such distinctions did not exist. The closer we can get to understanding the ancient mind within ourselves, the closer we can reconnect with the ideas embedded within the writings they left behind.

What is your first reaction to this picture? Is it one of horror or sorrow for these poor flood victims? How do you think the Mesopotamians themselves would have reacted to this scene? It may surprise you to learn that they would have interpreted this picture completely differently. They would have seen a depiction of the much-awaited flood season when the fertile floodwaters would replenish the land and its inhabitants, using traditional floatation devices, go about their business getting ready for the next growing season. This example highlights an important fact. In order to understand the ancient world, we must understand how the ancient peoples viewed their relationship to the environment. Doing so allows us to understand why ancient cultures developed a certain way and opens a window through which we can start to interpret the art and literature as its ancient creators once did.

3

Part One

A Hidden Past

"I now establish my covenant with you and your descendants after you." Genesis 9:9

Biblical Flood Tale
1000–600 BCE

We start our journey with a story that is familiar to most people—the biblical tale of Noah's ark and the Great Flood. It is the story of a creator, whom, angry at sinful humanity sends a flood to destroy humankind so that he can start over again. However, God instructs Noah, the only righteous man left, to build an *ark* and fill it with clean animals (livestock), unclean animals (wild animals), and the birds of the sky. After Noah completes this task, a great storm descends and the whole world is flooded, but Noah, his family, and the precious cargo of animals, are safe in the ark which floats on the swirling floodwaters. After some time, the ark eventually settles in the northeast amongst the mountains of *Ararat*. Noah, eager to learn if the floodwaters have receded, releases a raven that flies away and does not return. Noah then releases a dove that eventually returns with an olive branch in its beak, signaling that the flood is over. As a sign of his promise never to flood the world again, God sets a rainbow high in the sky.

Scholars agree that this inspiring tale was compiled in ancient Mesopotamia during the sixth century BCE from a variety of older sources, an idea that is part of the *documentary hypothesis*. However, as we shall see, these older sources were derived from an earlier version of a **Mesopotamian** flood tale that was originally compiled hundreds of years earlier.

Left: The biblical version of the flood tale displays many literary features consistent with Mesopotamian literature. It was likely authored by scholars from the Levant who were brought to Mesopotamia by the Babylonians to train as scribes. After the fall of the *Neo-Babylonian Empire* in 539 BCE, these scholars returned to the Levant and took with them many aspects of Mesopotamian culture, including the Great Flood tale. The story of Noah's Ark then found its way into the Jewish *Tanakh and* was later spread throughout the West in the biblical book of *Genesis when* Europe adopted Christianity.

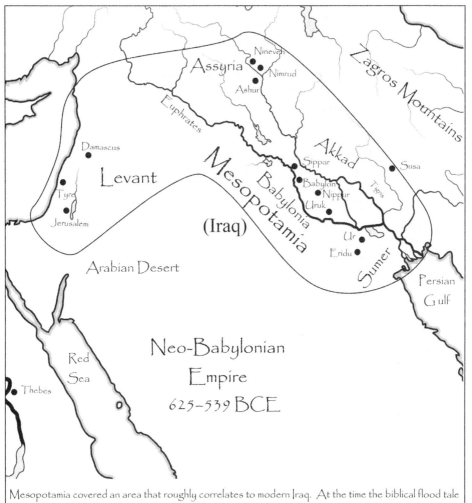

Mesopotamia covered an area that roughly correlates to modern Iraq. At the time the biblical flood tale was written, the region was dominated by the Neo-Babylonian Empire (625 – 539 BCE), stretching from the Mediterranean in the west to the Persian Gulf in the east. The area had a tradition of communicating various versions of the Great Flood tale that stretched back to at least 3000 BCE.

Gilgamesh Flood Tale
1500–1000 BCE

Prior to the Neo-Babylonian Empire, the Neo Assyrian Empire (911–609 BCE) dominated Mesopotamia and it is from their libraries that we find an earlier version of the Great Flood tale.

Embedded within a larger narrative called the ***Epic of Gilgamesh***, this earlier version of the Great Flood story was recorded on ***clay tablets*** during the seventh century BCE, although the narrative started to take form around 1500–1000 BCE. In this version, it is the Mesopotamian gods who decide to wipe out humankind and it is ***Ea***, the Babylonian god of water, not God, who warns the only righteous man left on earth, ***Utnapishtim***, of the coming flood. Ea then instructs Utnapishtim to build a large ark and fill it with "all the wild beasts and animals." It then rains for seven days and nights and the whole world is flooded, but Utnapishtim, his family, and the animals are safe aboard the ark. As in the biblical story, the ark eventually comes to rest upon a mountain in the northeast, but this time it is ***Mt. Nisir.*** Utnapishtim, eager to learn if the floodwaters have receded releases a dove and a swallow, both which return to the ark because, unlike the biblical version of the story, the flood is *not* yet over. Finally, Utnapishtim releases a raven, which does not return, thus signaling the *end of the flood*. For preserving "the seed of all living creatures" the Gods make Utnapishtim immortal. The similarities between this and the biblical version are striking, but what is even more telling is that the Gilgamesh Flood tale was written not in Assyrian but in ***Akkadian*** which is a clue on the next stop of our journey.

Right: Discovered in the ruins of the famed Library of the Assyrian King *Ashurbanipal* in *Nineveh*, this seventh-century BCE clay tablet (now housed in the British Museum) records part of the Epic of Gilgamesh. The flood tale it contains influenced the creation of the biblical flood story.

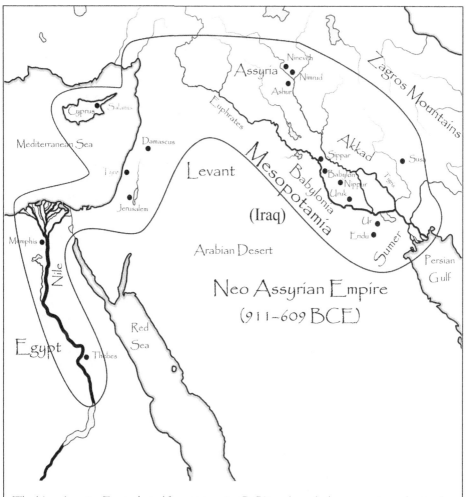

The Neo-Assyrian Empire lasted from 911 to 609 BCE and was the largest empire at the time. It stretched from Egypt in the west to Iran in the east. The capital, Nineveh, was home to the library of King Ashurbanipal and housed thousands of clay tablets including the Epic of Gilgamesh.

Akkadian Flood Tale
2500–1500 BCE

In 2334 BCE, Mesopotamia witnessed the development of one of the world's first empires. Formed through conquest by ambitious Akkadian Kings, the Akkadian Empire (2334–2160 BCE) is where we find an even older version of the Great Flood tale.

Part of a longer text, the ***Atra-Hasis Epic***, the Akkadian flood tale likely first originated sometime during the Akkadian period (2334–2154 BCE) and was developed over the next thousand years with various copies appearing during Old Babylonian (1894–1595 BCE), Middle Babylonian (1150 BCE–729 BCE), and the Assyrian (911–627 BCE) eras. The Akkadian version of the flood tale has striking similarities with the Gilgamesh version with both having gods deciding to send a flood to destroy humanity, however, the protagonist of the Akkadian flood tale is called ***Atra-Hasis***, and he is warned by a water god called ***Enki*** to build an ark for his family and fill it with livestock, the "wild beasts of the steppe," and all the birds of the sky. There follows a storm that lasts for seven days in which the whole world is flooded. Soon afterward, the flood recedes and Atra-Hasis, as was Utnapishtim, is made immortal by the gods.

Unfortunately, all the copies of the Atra-Hasis tale that have been found are missing segments and we don't have any passages describing the ark's landing on a mountain. And although one later version of a Middle Babylonian copy (found in ***Ugarit***) mentions the protagonist releasing a dove and "water bird," we do not know if the raven and swallow were included in the narrative. Despite this there is a hint to an even older version of the flood story; the god who warns Atra-Hasis (Enki), is not an Akkidian word but a Sumerian one, and this provides a tantalizing clue as to the story's final place of origin.

Left: Out of the dozens of fragments of the Epic of Atra-Hasis that have been found, one of the most complete is currently housed in the British Museum. Discovered in the Mesopotamian city of *Sipper,* it is dated to the 17 century BCE.

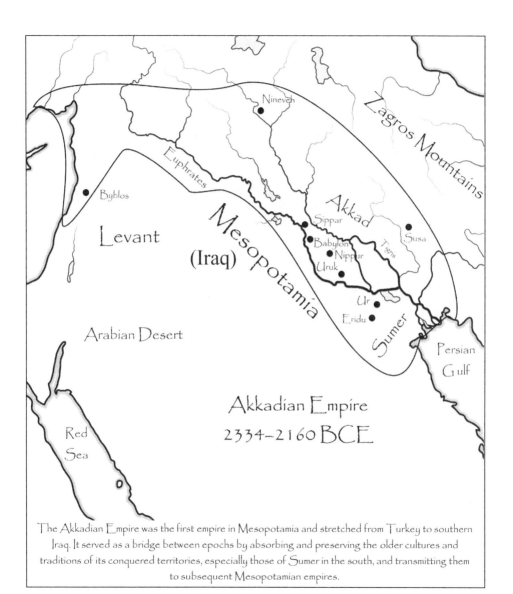

The Akkadian Empire was the first empire in Mesopotamia and stretched from Turkey to southern Iraq. It served as a bridge between epochs by absorbing and preserving the older cultures and traditions of its conquered territories, especially those of Sumer in the south, and transmitting them to subsequent Mesopotamian empires.

Sumerian Flood Tale
3000–2500 BCE

Nestled in the southern part of Iraq, close to the Persian Gulf, Sumer was one of the first civilizations in the world. Having been settled by 6000 BCE the region saw the development of the first written language around the 4th millennium BCE, and it is here that we find the earliest forms of literature.

One of these writings is the **Eridu Genesis**. Likely originating sometime between 3000–2500 BCE with some elements of the story probably being shared orally for some time before this, it includes the oldest known version of the Great Flood tale. Aptly called the Sumerian Flood tale, the clay tablet on which it is recorded is very damaged and only a small part is legible. However, there is enough surviving text to deduce that its plot is similar to that of the flood tale in the Epic of Atra-Hasis. Enki warns our hero, this time named **Ziusudra**, of the coming flood and tells him to build an ark. Unfortunately, the description of what was taken aboard the ark and its landing is missing. What we have instead, is an account of the conclusion of the flood, and this, alone, is very telling.

"Ziusudra then cut an opening in the Ark and Utu sent his light within. Then King Ziusudra stepped up before Utu kissing the ground before him and sacrificed bulls and countless numbers of sheep." Eridu Genesis

We can see in this passage that it is Utu (the Sumerian Sun God) who informs Ziusudra that the flood has receded. And in this version of the tale the ark never came to rest on a mountain nor were birds released to determine if the floodwaters had receded. We also see Ziusudra sacrificing many domestic animals to the gods, indicating that only Ziusudra's livestock was taken aboard.

Left: The Sumerian text called Eridu Genesis was found in the ancient city of *Nippur.* Kept at the University of Pennsylvania Museum, it is dated to the 16 century BCE although the narrative is believed to have originated in Sumer in the 3rd millennium BCE.

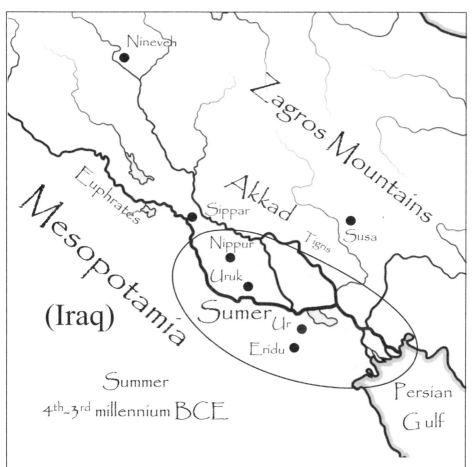

Nineveh

Zagros Mountains

Euphrates

Akkad

Mesopotamia

Sippar

Nippur

Tigris

Susa

Uruk

(Iraq)

Sumer

Ur

Eridu

Summer

4th-3rd millennium BCE

Persian

Gulf

Mesopotamian tradition held that the Sumerian city of Eridu was the first city in the world and excavations of the site confirm that a settlement was firmly established by at least 5000 BCE. The city was originally a fishing town on the coast of the Persian Gulf and was dedicated to the water god Enki (of the flood tale) who was believed to reside at its main temple. Over time, silting caused by the Euphrates and Tigris rivers, had moved the coast eastward over 100 miles and, eventually, Eridu lost its access to the sea.

An Ancient Heritage
The Development of an Idea

As we have seen, during its long history the Great Flood tale underwent many changes. (See Appx. 5, p.85 for a list of all discovered flood tablets.) This is hardly surprising, especially the differences in the protagonist's name, reasons for the flood, names of mountains the ark landed on, and the cast of gods involved. It is only expected that the various ancient societies that adopted the story would seek to communicate the narrative in a cultural context that its people could relate to.

However, there is a second group of differences between the various versions that do not appear to have been influenced by differing cultural considerations. These include elements such as the class of animals taken aboard, the ark's landing, and the methods of determining the end of the flood. These differences are concerned with developing the underlying plot and, once introduced, were generally accepted or developed by the authors of later versions of the story. This begs the question, *what influenced the development of the plot and what purpose did it serve?*

As we will learn later, the plot development was not accidental nor inconsequential. In fact, it provides important clues as to the origin of the tale and its hidden message. That is because those who developed the flood tale were communicating hidden ideas about their conception

of a cosmos that was constantly changing. To fully understand those ideas, we first need to explore the influences that shaped their understanding of the cosmos and their methods of expression.

Left: Enki (Ea in Akkadian) was the Mesopotamian god of water. He is a very ancient god and was associated with the city of Eridu. Often depicted holding an overflowing jar, (representing celestial floodwaters), he is the god who warns the protagonist in the first three versions of the flood tale. In the biblical version of the flood tale, Enki is replaced by God.

Development of the Flood Tale

By comparing the similarities and differences of the various versions of the Mesopotamian flood tale we can see how the plot developed over time.

Biblical Flood Tale
1000 - 600 BCE

God warns Noah of coming flood
Noah fills ark with clean & unclean animals (livestock & wild animals) and birds
Rains for forty days and nights
Ark lands on mountain
Noah releses a raven that does not return
Noah releases a dove that returns
God places a rainbow in the sky

Gilgamesh Flood Story
Epic of Gilgamesh
1500 - 1000 BCE

Ea warns Utnapishtim of the coming flood
Utnapishtim fills ark with livestock, wild animals, and birds
Rains for seven days and nights
Ark lands on mountain
Utnapishtim releases a swallow and dove that returns
Utnapishtim releases a raven that does not return
Utnapishtim is made immortal

Akkadian Version
Epic of Atra-Hasis
2500 - 1500 BCE

Enki warns Atra-Hasis of the coming flood
Atra-Hasis fills ark with livestock, wild animals, and birds
Rains for seven days and nights
Ark lands on mountain *
Atra-Hasis releases a dove and a "water bird"*
Atra-Hasis is made immortal

Summerian Version
Eridu Genesis
3000 - 2500 BCE

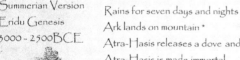

Enki warns Ziusudra of the coming flood
Ziusudra builds an ark and fills it with livestock
Rains for seven days and nights
Sun god Uutu informs Ziusudra flood is over
Ziusudra is made immortal

*The addition of the ark landing on the mountain and the releasing of birds likely started to appear in the later Akkadian versions of the tale.

A depiction of exiles in Babylon. Neuville. 1867.

Part Two

The Art of Story Telling

"Strange things have been spoken, why does your heart speak strangely?"- The Epic of Gilgamesh

Cosmic Beginnings
The Foundation of Civilization

The worldview of the authors who composed the various flood tales was vastly different to our own. The cosmos in the Mesopotamian mind was a place where all events were seemly interrelated, and a world where these relationships were expressed through various signs. Nowhere was this truer than in the belief that the appearance and positions of the stars throughout the year could signal events on Earth.

Such a philosophy had its roots with the rise of ancient agriculture. The farming of cereal crops in Mesopotamia started to appear around 9000 BCE and one of the earliest challenges faced by these early farmers was knowing when to sow and harvest crops. They solved this problem by turning to the stars. *Neolithic* Mesopotamians soon learned to recognize clusters or groups of stars and correlate their appearance and position in the night sky with the correct time to engage in various agricultural activities. Believing that the appearance of stars or *constellations* also had an influence over the success of their crops, the art of astrology became a fundamental part of early Mesopotamian culture and was passed orally from one generation to the next.

However, ancient astronomy underwent a rapid development when the success of farming gave rise to the first civilizations and the development of the first written languages. This allowed the names of constellations and planetary movements to be recorded on clay tablets, eventually allowing for a more organized approached to astronomy. The practice soon became a complex art form reserved for the priestly classes. By 2000 BCE, Ziggurat temples started to appear across Mesopotamia (see Appx. 4, p. 84) which employed hundreds of priests whose primary purpose was to observe and record the appearance and movements of the planets and the stars every night.

By the sixth century BCE (the time the biblical version of the flood tale was compiled) Mesopotamia had a sophisticated body of astronomical knowledge that included observations stretching back many millennia.

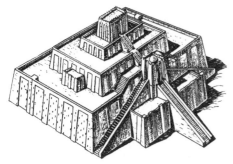

Left: By 2000 BCE, Ziggurats such as these were part of large temple complexes that were scattered across Mesopotamia. It was here that hundreds of priests recorded the time of a star or constellation's rising as well as its position throughout the night in an attempt to interpret what the cosmos was communicating.

Right: The Mesopotamians used water clocks to keep track of time throughout the night. Although no examples of these water clocks have survived, the diagram on the right shows its principal. A unit of time is measured by how long it takes a known quantity of water to drain from a container. With this, the position of a star throughout the night could be measured against time.

	SUMERIAN (Vertical)	SUMERIAN (Rotated)	EARLY BABYLONIAN	LATE BABYLONIAN	ASSYRIAN
star					
sun					
month					
man					
king					
son					
head					
lord					
his					
reed					
power					
mouth					
ox					
bird					
destiny					

Left: An example of the development of Mesopotamian wedge markings used to record information on clay tablets. Called cuneiform, it was first developed by the Sumerians in the 4th millennium BCE and was later adopted and developed by the Akkadians, Babylonians, and Assyrians, allowing the transmission of astronomical observations throughout these eras.

Voices from the Past
Recreating the Cosmos

Fortunately for us, many of the astronomical observations recorded by the Mesopotamians throughout their history have survived, providing a fascinating insight into how their understanding of the cosmos evolved over time. Clay tablets have been discovered that record information about the names of stars and constellations, their position in the sky, and the timing of their appearance as well as their theological importance (see Appx. 7, p. 93).

One of the most important texts to survive is called the ***Mul.Apin*** (see Appx. 6 p. 86). Originally composed around 1100 BCE, one part lists the names of Mesopotamian constellations and their position in relation to one another. Astrological texts such as the Mul.Apin preserved knowledge of these constellations for future generations of Mesopotamian priests so it should not be surprising, that many constellations remained consistent through most of Mesopotamian history.

Later, Mesopotamian astronomy was adopted by the ancient Greeks following the conquest of ***Alexandra the Great*** and it spread throughout the Hellenized world from Egypt to as far as India (see Appx. 2 p. 82).

Using surviving Mesopotamian texts and ancient Hellenic and Egyptian sources based on Mesopotamian astronomy (see Appx. 9 and 10, p. 97-98), we can build up a picture of how the night sky appeared to the ancient Mesopotamians. Although we are not entirely certain how the Mesopotamians visualized some constellations, researchers have recreated ancient star charts using traditional artwork to give us a sense of how the Mesopotamians saw the night sky.

Left: A clay tablet called the Mul.Apin currently located at the British Museum. It was discovered in the remains of the Library of King Ashurbanipal during the 19 century and lists numerous Mesopotamian constellations. Written in Akkadian, it dates to the 7th century BCE, but the astronomical observations it records where made around 1100 BCE.

Reconstruction of the Mesopotamian Night Sky 1100 BCE

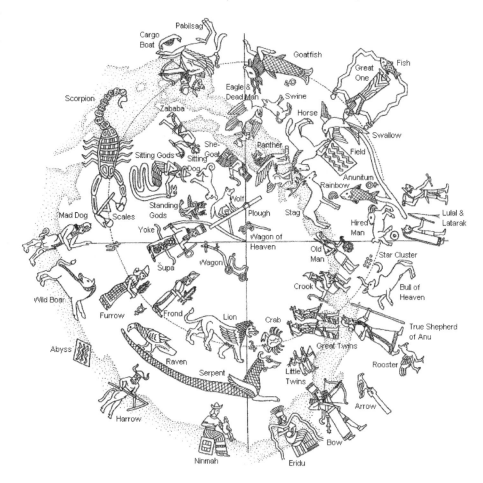

The above reconstructed star chart is taken from "Babylonian Star-Lore. An Illustrated Guide to the Star-Lore and Constellations of Ancient Babylonia," Gavin White, Solaria Publications, 2014.

Pillars of Time
The Narrative Above

As civilization and agriculture developed and became more complex, so did their constellations. As "celestial messages" that had allowed agriculture and, ultimately, civilization to develop, the most important heavenly signals were those that indicated the correct time for certain agricultural activities or provided a commentary about the workings and structure of the cosmos. By 1500 BCE, many Mesopotamian constellations had developed into their final form and provided a divine narrative to the activities taking place below.

This celestial narrative was structured around four main points, the spring and fall equinoxes and the summer and winter solstices. Together, these four points represented the pillars that supported the yearly cycle. The spring equinox was used to indicate the arrival of spring and the spring floods (see Appx. 3 p. 83). It was celebrated by an agricultural festival called *Akitu*. Over time, Mesopotamian constellations that became associated with the spring equinox included the Bull of Heaven (representing the plowing of the fields), the Hired Man (representing hired farm laborers and sheep), and the Crook (representing a shepherd tending to the newborn lambs).

The summer solstice was associated with death and famine, as the hot summer sun scorched the earth and yellowed the vegetation. It was celebrated by remembrance of the death of the god of vegetation and fertility, *Dumuzi*. Mesopotamian constellations associated with this period include the Lion (representing the hot summer sun), the Serpent (representing drought and death), and the Crab (representing the entrance to the underworld).

The fall equinox marked the second half of the year and was associated with sowing and reseeding. Mesopotamian constellations, which appeared just before this event, include the Frond and Furrow (representing reseeding), the Harrow (representing plowing), and the Raven (representing the fertile rains).

The winter solstice took place during the rainy season and represented the death and rebirth of the sun. Frequent storms replenished the scorched earth and dried vegetation, and it was at this part of the year that the Mesopotamians celebrated the rebirth of Dumuzi, the vegetation god. As a time when the powers of rebirth were understood to be at their strongest, the winter solstice was also a period when Mesopotamians believed that the souls of the dead made their way back up to heaven. Constellations that dominated the sky during this time included those that were associated with storms, such as the Great One which represented the overflowing celestial waters. There were also constellations, such as Pabilsag, that represented Mesopotamian ancestors guiding the dead on the start of their journey into the next world.

It should come as no surprise, given the importance of astronomy, that the Mesopotamian psyche sought to express the heavens in almost all aspects of their culture. In particular, the use of metaphor in creating and naming constellations found its way into early myths through the form of allegory, and would eventually influence the development of some of the earliest pieces of literature.

Left: The constellation called the Furrow was the predecessor to the modern constellation Virgo. It was portrayed as a goddess holding a barley stalk and would rise in the autumn during the barley reseeding period. The development of constellations such as these were originally focused on the timing of certain agricultural activities.

Right. The constellation Pabilsag, which represented ancestors, is the predecessor to the modern constellation Sagittarius. Over time some constellations, such as this one, moved away from their agricultural origins and took on a more philosophical tone about the nature of life and death.

Beyond the Narrative
Divine Reflections

We can see the influence of astrology in one of the first and oldest pieces of

literature ever written. Called the Epic of Gilgamesh, it was originally five separate poems originating from Sumer sometime around the 3rd millennium BCE. In the epic, there is a passage that describes the Sumerian goddess ***Inanna*** unleashing the Bull of Heaven so that it can descend to Earth to ravish the land and cause a famine. Because of the surviving astronomical texts, we now know that the goddess Inanna represented the planet Venus, and that the Bull of Heaven represented a Mesopotamian constellation of the same name that corresponded with the modern constellation of Taurus. Understanding this, we can see that the passage of Inanna unleashing the celestial bull is actually an allegory expressing the belief that if the planet Venus crossed the constellation Taurus then it signaled that a famine would occur across the land. This belief likely reflected the fact that, during the period the epic was written, Venus would transit across the constellation of Taurus in May, just before the start of the hot summer season that was typified by drought and the death of all vegetation.

Above: Gilgamesh, who was often depicted strangling a lion, was the protagonist of the Epic of Gilgamesh.

These poems contain many other astronomical allegories and allusions, and the texts' importance ensured their endurance, even after successive empires dominated the region, eventually being developed into a single narrative about an ancient King called ***Gilgamesh*** and his quest for immortality. By the 11th century BCE, the Gilgamesh version of the Great Flood tale was added to the epic's narrative as part of a scene when Gilgamesh meets Utnapishtim who relates the story of the Great Flood and his subsequent gift of immortality.

Allegorical Characters in the Epic of Gilgamesh

The Bull of Heaven mentioned in the Epic of Gilgamesh represents a constellation that would later become known as Taurus.

The goddess Inanna represented the planet Venus. She was often depicted with rays of light emanating from her back, a reference to the fact that the planet Venus was one of the brightest objects in the night sky.

In the Epic of Gilgamesh, the sun god Utu helps Gilgamesh defeat the monster Humbaba. Often depicted with rays of light emerging from his back, Utu represented the sun, and it was his rays of light that signaled to Ziusudra that the flood was over in the earliest versions of the Great Flood tale.

In one passage of the Epic of Gilgamesh there is a description of a "scorpion man" whose job is to guard the entrance to the underworld. At the time this passage was added to the Epic of Gilgamesh (2000-1000 BCE), the fall equinox, believed to mark the start of the sun's journey into the underworld, took place in the constellation called the Scorpion.

Magical Metaphors
The Art of Allegory

As the art of astrology developed, the use of allegory to express celestial observations became widely used in a genre of literature known as ***omen texts***. Many of these texts were concerned with the interpretation of astronomical events. One famous text is called the Enuma Anu Enlil (EAE). Made up of over 70 tablets, it lists hundreds celestial observations in allegoric form. An example of the type of allegories it includes is:

"If the Fish stands next to the Raven: fish and fowl will thrive."

In this allegory the "Fish" refers to the Mesopotamian constellation, called the Goatfish and the Raven is a reference to the planet Mercury. The omen is saying if the planet Mercury appears in the constellation of the Goatfish, there will be an abundance of food.

Astronomical information such as the Enuma Anu Enlil was jealously guarded by astrologers, and tablets have been found warning students of the art not to reveal their knowledge to outsiders, usually under the punishment of death.

Despite the secrecy surrounding the use of astrological allegory, we should not be surprised, given its importance and widespread use, to find it hidden just below the surface of almost every aspect of Mesopotamian culture.

Left: Throughout much of Mesopotamian history the type of astrology practiced was ***mundane astrology*** and was only used for predicting the fortunes of a nation or a king. Besides the use of texts such as the Enuma Anu Enlil, various texts called the *commentaries* (see Appx. 7, p. 93) were used to help astrologers understand the metaphors and allegories employed in predictions.

Birth of a Celestial Omen

Clay tablets discovered in the remains of the Library of Ashurbanipal give us a fascinating insight into the type of processes involved in the creation of an omen and the importance astrologers gave to preserving historical astronomical observations.

Left: A clay tablet that was part of a daily diary. These recorded daily celestial events that were unusual or deemed important.

Right: A clay tablet that was part of a monthly summary. These were summaries of important celestial observations of a particular month. They were created using information from daily diaries.

Left: A clay tablet from the Enuma Anu Enlil (EAE). The omens contained in the EAE were created by attempting to correlate past observations from texts such as the monthly summaries to subsequent events taking place on earth.

"If the moon wears a crown ...."

Right: Some tablets contained warnings to astrologers not to share their interpretations of the celestial allegories to outsiders, otherwise they would be punished by the gods.

Hidden in Plain Sight
Heavenly Characters

Once we are aware of some of the dominant literary influences in Mesopotamia, reexamining the Great Flood tale becomes exciting. Armed with our knowledge of Mesopotamian astronomy, we notice that elements of the flood tale are also Mesopotamian stars or constellations. Some of these elements are obvious. There are ancient constellations called the Raven, Swallow, and Rainbow. A constellation known as the Lion represented the "wild beasts of the field," and the Bull of Heaven represented the livestock that was taken aboard the ark in the earliest stories of the flood.

The flood waters are present, too, in the form of the Milky Way, believed by Mesopotamians to be part of the fertile waters of Heaven.

But what of the ark, the mountain, and the dove? Where do they fit into the night sky? These elements of the flood tale are present as well, but to find them we need to understand a special type of literary technique—***metonymy.***

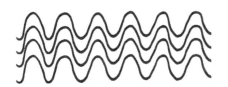

Above: The Mesopotamians often described the sky as being made of water to explain the fertile rains during the rainy season and the Milky Way was often associated with a celestial ocean or river. Some Mesopotamian myths go even further and describe how the Milky Way was created from the tail of a saltwater goddess known as Tiamat.

Below: Known as the Bull of Heaven, this constellation was one of the oldest, first represented in Mesopotamian art in the 5th millennium BCE. It is now known as the constellation of Taurus.

The Rainbow

Associated with the Mesopotamian god *Harriru*, the Rainbow represented the fertile rains of heaven and was seen a positive symbol. It was located just above the modern constellation Pisces.

The Lion

The Mesopotamian name for this constellation means "large carnivore," which was a term they used to refer to predators and wild animals. The constellation also symbolized the summer sun and the King.

The Raven

The Raven constellation was associated with the Mesopotamian storm and rain god *Adad* and represented fertile rainwaters. It was in the same part of the sky as the modern constellation Corvus.

The Swallow

Associated with water and fish, the Swallow represented the rainy season. It was located where the present day Pisces constellation lies.

Mysterious Metonymy
Making Connections

The use of Metonymy is a curious but common feature of Mesopotamian literature. In particular, the substitution of a celestial body's identity with an associated object or idea was a common technique and Mesopotamian astrological texts contain hundreds of cases. For example, the planet Mars is rarely mentioned by its actual name but, because the planet was associated with wolves and foxes, astrologers would instead refer to it as the wolf or fox.

Once we understand this technique of indirectly referring to a star or constellation by use of its associations, we can start to find the missing elements of the flood tale in the night sky.

To find the mountain mentioned in the flood tale, we turn to the constellation of Supa. This group of stars represented the Mesopotamian god **Enlil,** and was located in the space occupied by the present-day constellation called Bootes. In Mesopotamian religion, Enlil's title was the Great Mountain. His constellation included the brightest star in the night sky, Arcturus. It was

Supa

Great Mountain

believed to be part of a great celestial peak and so this constellation can be referred to as the mountain.

The way that the ancient astronomers used these associations could sometimes be very complex. For example, a constellation known as the "Great One" was associated with the **kidneys.** However the constellation called the Star of Eridu was also associated with the kidneys.

Using the common association of the kidney, astrologers would associate the constellation called "the Great One" with the Star of Eridu (Star of Eridu = kidney = Great One). Complicating things further, many constellations could have more than one association.

This naturally could become very confusing and so astrological texts written for kings would often be provided with notes of explanation. Besides hiding the true meaning of texts, metonymy also provided a level of flexibility in crafting and interpreting the allegories that were created.

By using this technique of shared associations, we find the dove through the constellation of Anunitum. This constellation was considered by Mesopotamians to be an aspect of the goddess Inanna who was represented by many symbols, one of which was the dove.

Anunitum   Inanna   Dove

Left: The dove, through its relationship with Inanna, can be associated with the constellation Anunitum.

But what about the most enigmatic, inspiring, but elusive element of all—the ark? It turns out the ark was sitting in plain view all the time, veiled by the use of metonymy behind the celestial object known as the Star of Eridu. This star was associated with Enki who, being the patron god of the fishing settlement of Eridu, was associated with boats and water and, so, later became associated with the creation of the ark. Later Greek and Egyptian sources (see Appx. 9 & 10, p. 97-98) which were based on Mesopotamian astronomy, continued to echo the idea that the Star of Eridu was associated with floods and ships.

The ark, through its relationship with Enki, can be associated with the constellation called the Star of Eridu.

Star of Eridu   Enki   Ark

After having identified all the plot elements of the Great Flood story as metaphors for celestial objects, the next questions are, what did all these constellations have in common, and how did they come together to create the flood story narrative? In order to answer these questions, we need to focus on one special time of the Mesopotamian year—the winter solstice.

31

Winter Skies
A Celestial Stage

The time around the winter solstice was special in Mesopotamia for it occurred during the rainy season, when the much-awaited storms would provide relief from the hot summer season.

This was also the only time of year that the constellations and celestial bodies that represent elements of the Great Flood tale—the ark, flood waters, animals, mountain, raven, swallow, dove, and rainbow—all appeared in the heavens at the same time.

But how can we be sure that the appearance of these constellations during the winter solstice is significant? Well, if we compare the timeline of when these constellations were created, and their subsequence movements across the heavens with the timeline of the development of the various flood stories, something truly remarkable happens. But before we explore this fascinating process, we first need to examine how constellations move through the sky and the methods used to measure their position.

Great One

Left: In Mesopotamia, the winter solstice was associated with storms. Around 4000 BCE the winter solstice sun would appear in a group of stars that would later become the water constellation called the "Great One." He was often represented holding an overflowing jar, representing the celestial waters pouring down to earth.

Goatfish

Right: By 2000 BCE, the winter solstice sun started to appear in another constellation associated with water, called the Goatfish. The watery nature of these constellations, and their shifting positions through the night sky during the winter solstices, provided a cosmic backdrop in which the Great flood tale could unfold.

Mesopotamian Constellations Associated with Storms and Flooding

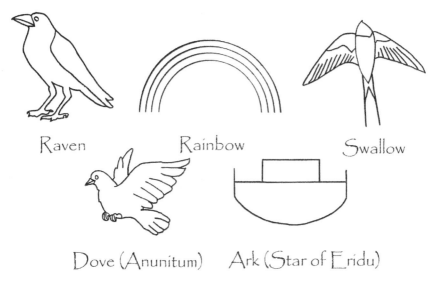

Raven   Rainbow   Swallow

Dove (Anunitum)   Ark (Star of Eridu)

Above: The constellations that found expression in the Great Flood narrative would all appear on the same night in the southern sky of Mesopotamia during the winter solstice. The Mesopotamian winter was the rainy season and, as a result, these constellations were associated with water and flooding.

Right: The constellation that represented the mountain in the flood tale (Supa) was also visible in the night sky during the winter solstice. However, instead of appearing in the southern sky with the other Great Flood constellations, it would appear in the northeastern part of the heavens.

Great Mountain

Part Three

Celestial Mechanics

"Measure what is measurable and make measurable what is not so." – Galileo Galilei

Divine Circle
The Shape of Creation

The night sky has fascinated our ancestors since the dawn of time. However, questions about the true nature of the stars and their movements across the heavens were approached differently by different peoples. But, behind these questions, ancient humans held the same cosmological assumptions about the divine nature of the heavens. For the celestial space above our heads is dominated by the most fundamental of all shapes—the circle. From the shape of the sun and the moon to the stars, planets, and their circular orbits, the circle is the ultimate expression of the cosmos. Indeed, ancient peoples saw within the circle the idea of cosmic unity, a divine expression that was inherent within the very shape of the universe itself. We can still appreciate this wonder ourselves, for if we were to stand beneath the night sky and visualize the location of the modern *zodiac*, we would notice constellations emerging from the eastern horizon arch above us and disappear below the western horizon, creating a semi-circular path. If we could somehow continue to follow the path made by the zodiac below the horizon, we would notice more constellations creating an arch below us and forming a complete circle.

Aries the Ram   Cancer the Crab   Libra the Scales   Capricorn the Goat

Taurus the Bull   Leo the Lion   Scorpio the Scorpion   Aquarius the Water-Bearer

Gemini the Twins   Virgo the Maiden   Sagittarius the Archer   Pisces the Fishes

Above: There are twelve special western constellations that together are called the zodiac.

The zodiac constellations form a circle in the sky, and in ancient times, formed the boundary of the cosmos.

A Celestial Mirror
Sacred Images

If the zodiac circle represents the boundaries of the cosmos, then within it we find the symbols of creation—other constellations that represent the world of humans and their religious myths.

This is because the ancient mind saw the sky as a divine window, and the zodiac circle, constellations, and planets above served as a conduit through which the cosmos could reflect events taking place down below. These insights reflected the ancient mind's remarkable ability to observe and understand subtle changes in their environment. From the sun's creation of the seasons to the moon's effect on the tide of the seas and the planets gravitational pulls on the Earth's spin and orbit, the heavenly bodies really do exert an influence on the world around us.

Below: An example of some of the *traditional constellations* that can be found inside the zodiac circle. The development of many of these constellations were influenced by ancient Greek myths, underlining the ancient belief in the divine nature of stars.

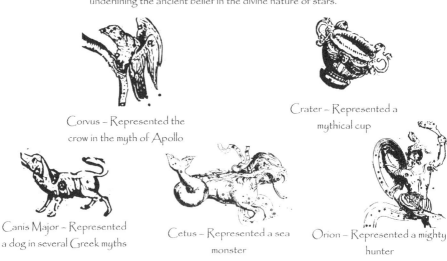

Corvus – Represented the crow in the myth of Apollo

Crater – Represented a mythical cup

Canis Major – Represented a dog in several Greek myths

Cetus – Represented a sea monster

Orion – Represented a mighty hunter

The zodiac circle is full of constellations which represent the world of humankind and their myths.

Daily Dance
The Sidereal Day

The ancients realized that nothing is stationary in nature. Movement is everywhere and is a fundamental part of the universe. Nowhere is this truer than in the celestial space above our heads. If we were to observe the zodiac circle for long enough, after a while we would notice the whole circle and its contents moving very slowly, spinning from east to west. During this rotation, a constellation after one revolution would arrive back at its original position in approximately 23 hours, 56 minutes, a unit of time called a *sidereal day*.

Above: The zodiac circle and the constellations within it slowly rotate, completing a revolution in approximately 23 hrs. 56 minutes. Here, the constellation Aries is at the top of the zodiac circle at 0 hours.

Left: The constellation Aries approximately 11hrs. 58 mins later at the bottom of the zodiac circle.

Aries after 23 hrs. 56 mins.

Aries after 11 hrs. 58 mins.

Right: The constellation Aries depicted another 11 hrs. 58 mins later at its original starting position. The time it took to complete the revolution is called a sidereal day.

Light and Dark
The Seen and Unseen

Only about half the zodiac circle ever looks down on the world at any given moment. That is because the horizon obscures its lower half. However, the zodiac constellations have a privileged position, for the circle they form is the path that the sun travels across the sky on.

Every day the sun rises in the east within a zodiac constellation, reaching its highest point at noon, and then descends westward before disappearing below the horizon. During this time, the constellations are invisible in the bright light of the sun. But after the sun dips below the horizon, the zodiac and constellations become visible to the world below.

At night, the sun continues its circular path below the horizon, this time traveling eastward to rise again in the morning. It takes about 24 hours for the sun to appear in the same position in the sky as it did the previous day, a unit of time known as a *solar day.*

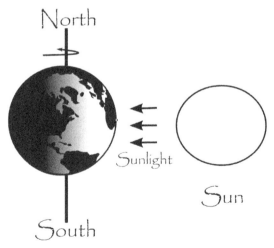

The apparent motion of the sun across the sky is caused by the earth spinning on its axis. As seen from earth, it takes approximately 24 hours for the sun to complete a revolution.

East   South   West

Only about half the zodiac circle is above the horizon at any given moment.

East   South   West

The sun rises within the constellation of Aries.

Morning

East   South   West

The sun at noon traveling westward within the constellation Aries

Noon

East   South   West

The sun setting with Aries in the west. The sun will continue its circular path below the horizon within the constellation of Aries

Evening

A Yearly Dance
The Solar Journey

The position of the sun is not fixed within the zodiac circle. You may have noticed that it takes the sun approximately four minutes longer to complete a revolution compared to a constellation. The time difference between a sidereal day and a solar day occurs because the earth is orbiting the sun. The sun, which is much closer to the earth than the stars, changes its position relative to the earth faster than that of the constellations. Because of this, the sun takes slightly longer to revisit the same local **meridian** than it does a constellation. The effect created for an observer on the ground is that, as the sun travels across the sky, it appears to slowly lag the constellations in the zodiac circle. In approximately a month, the sun rises and sets within a completely new zodiac constellation. The sun continues this apparent drift leftward within the zodiac circle throughout the year taking 12 months to travel through all 12 constellations. This completes a *solar year*, which is the amount of time it takes for the sun to return to the same position within a previous constellation, and is approximately 365 days.

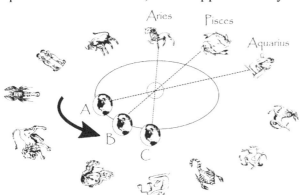

Left: The earth orbits the sun. As it does so, the sun's daily position within the zodiac circle slowly shifts leftward. At point A, the sun rises and sets within Aquarius. By point B, it rises and sets within Pisces and by point C, it rises and sets within Aries.

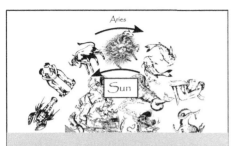

Aries

East   South   West

The sun rises in Aries. It takes the sun approximately four minutes longer to complete a revolution then the zodiac constellations.

April - May

Taurus

East   South   West

The slower moving sun is shifting left through the zodiac. In May, it rises in the constellation of Taurus.

May - June

Virgo

East   South   West

After a further four months, the sun rises and sets within Virgo.

September - October

Pisces

East   South   West

Six months later, the sun rises in Pisces. In one more month, it will have traveled through all twelve constellations starting again in Aries.

March - April

Highs and Lows
Summer and Winter

If we were to observe the sun's path within the zodiac circle throughout the year, we would notice that its height above the horizon changes constantly. In summer, the sun appears to travel across the sky higher above the horizon than it does in winter. This is because the earth's axis is tilted approximately 23.5 degrees from its **orbital plane.** So as the earth orbits the sun, there will be moments in the year when the earth is tilted either toward or away from the sun. In the northern hemisphere, the earth's maximum tilt *toward* the sun happens in June and is called the *summer solstice*. On this day, the sun travels across the sky at its highest point above the horizon. Likewise, the earth's maximum tilt *away* from the sun happens in December and is called the *winter solstice*. On this day, the sun travels across the sky at its lowest point above the horizon.

To measure the height of the sun above the horizon we take the earth's **equator** and project it out into space to create a celestial equator. We can then measure the angular distance of the sun north or south of the celestial equator. This measurement is called *declination* and is abbreviated DEC.

Summer Solstice   Winter Solstice

In the northern hemisphere, the sun and zodiac circle appear higher in the sky as the earth tilts toward the sun during the summer. They appear at their lowest as the earth tilts away from the sun during the winter.

By projecting the earth's equator into space, we create the celestial equator which is designated as 0+. Circles indicating the angular distance above or below the celestial equator can then be displayed. Mesopotamians would measure a star's declination with reference to a fixed object such a building or mountain.

46

Summer and Winter Solstice

Right: By visualizing the lines of declination across the sky, we can measure the height of the sun above the horizon. During the summer solstice, the sun reaches a maximum declination of +23.5 above the celestial equator while in the constellation of Gemini.

Summer Solstice in June

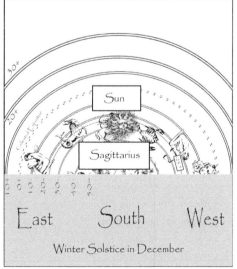

Winter Solstice in December

Left: During the winter solstice, the sun reaches its lowest point above the horizon with a DEC of -23.5 below the celestial equator while in the constellation of Sagittarius. Throughout the year the sun is constantly moving between these two extremes (+23.5/-23.5).

An Equal Division
Spring and Fall

As the sun descends from its highest point during the summer solstice to its lowest point during the winter solstice, there will be a point when it crosses the celestial equator. As it does so, the earth will be leaning neither toward nor away from the sun. When this happens, the length of night and day are of the same length. This event occurs in September and is called the *fall equinox* and marks the beginning of the fall. After the winter solstice, the sun begins to rise again from its lowest point on its way toward its highest point during the summer solstice. Again, it will cross the celestial equator and, again, the length of night and day will be equal. This take place in March and is called the *spring equinox,* marking the beginning of spring.

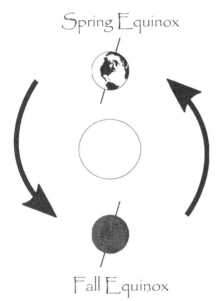

Spring Equinox

Fall Equinox

Left: During its orbit, the earth will normally be in a state of transition between leaning toward or away from the sun. However, there will be two moments when the earth's axis will be leaning neither toward nor away from the sun, but, instead, will face it vertically. Called the equinox, this happens in March and September and marks the beginning of spring and fall respectively. During the equinoxes, the sun appears to rise and travel along the celestial equator. Together, the summer and winter solstices and the spring and autumn equinoxes create the four seasons and were seen by Mesopotamians as fundamental points in the structure of the cosmos.

Spring and Fall Equinoxes

Right: During the spring equinox, the sun travels along the celestial equator (dotted line) with a declination of 0+ while in the constellation of Pisces.

Spring Equinox in March

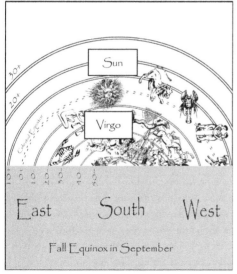

Fall Equinox in September

Left: During the fall equinox, the sun travels along the celestial equator (dotted line) with a declination of 0+ while in the constellation of Virgo.

An Orderly Progression
The Nightly March

When observing the constellations, it is useful to express their lateral position in the sky in relation to a fixed reference point. The reference that is used is the position of the sun as it crosses the celestial equator during the spring equinox. We can use this point to measure the constellations angular distance eastward along the celestial equator. This angular distance is called the *right ascension* (abbreviated as RA) and its unit of measure is in hours.

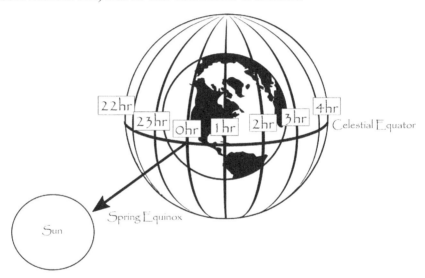

Above: Right Ascension can be thought of as the earth's longitudes being projected out into space and is measured from the sun at the spring equinox. Moving eastward at 15-degree intervals, each celestial longitude is called an hour and the celestial grid has 24 hours. The position of the constellations as they travel across the sky can be measured using its right ascension. While the sun's position with reference to its right ascension changes throughout the year, the right ascension of the constellations remains constant. Mesopotamians could measure a stars lateral position in a similar way, noting its position at certain times of the night for any given date.

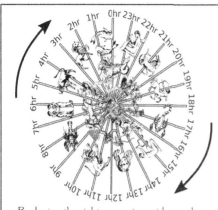

By laying the right ascension grid over the zodiac circle, we see each constellation has a position referenced as its right ascension.

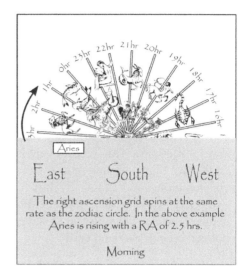

East   South   West

The right ascension grid spins at the same rate as the zodiac circle. In the above example Aries is rising with a RA of 2.5 hrs.

Morning

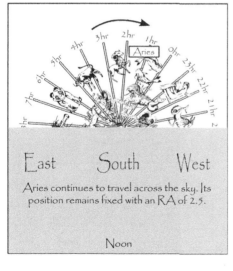

East   South   West

Aries continues to travel across the sky. Its position remains fixed with an RA of 2.5.

Noon

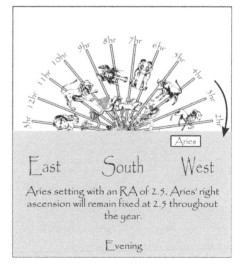

East   South   West

Aries setting with an RA of 2.5. Aries' right ascension will remain fixed at 2.5 throughout the year.

Evening

51

Mystical Wobble
The Secret Cycle

During a person's lifetime, night after night, season after season, and year after year, the constellations and fixed stars appear in the night sky at predictable times and positions, reflecting an orderly and stable cosmos. This cycle is due to the generally stable movement of the earth around its axis and its orbital path.

However, the earth has a hidden cycle that can only be noticed over several lifetimes. This secret cycle is called *precession*, and is caused by the earth wobbling around its own axis. This wobble, which causes the constellations and stars to shift their position within the night sky, is extremely slow. It takes approximately 26,000 years to complete one full cycle. However, it only takes several thousand years for its effects to be noticed by observers on earth.

The Effects of Precession

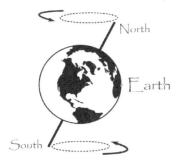

Above: Precession is the wobble of the earth around its own axis. It is caused by the gravitational pull of nearby planets. It takes about 26,000 years for the earth to complete one full wobble.

Above: By combining declination (DEC) with the right ascension (RA), we create the celestial sphere. This grid can be used to see the effects of precession more clearly.

52

Effects of Precession

Right: By laying the celestial sphere over the night sky, we can plot the position of the constellations. In the example on the right, the sun is setting within the constellation Sagittarius (RA 19hr & DEC -23.5) during the 2020 winter solstice.

Winter Solstice 2020

Winter Solstice 3020

Left: A thousand years later, during the 3020 winter solstice. The earth's precession causes Sagittarius's RA to shift forward so that it now has an RA of 20.5hr. The sun now sets in the constellation of Scorpio instead.

Death and Rebirth
An Act of Creation

As the earth continues its slow wobble, one obvious effect is that the sun appears to shift the summer and winter solstices, as well as the spring and fall equinoxes, backward through the zodiac circle, so that they take place within different constellations.

The earth's precession also causes the many constellations within the zodiac circle to slowly shift their orientation and position within the sky and in relation to one another. Within a few thousand years, it appears that the whole structure of the old cosmos has been destroyed with a new celestial heaven taking its place.

As we will learn, this celestial process was first realized by Mesopotamian astrologers while they poured over records of historical observations in an attempt to decipher what the heavens were communicating to the. Considered sacred knowledge about the divine workings of the cosmos, the precession of constellations was likely only known by a select number of high priest astrologers who expressed it through allegory to keep the secret safe from the uninitiated. In doing so they created some of the world's and most enduring pieces of literature.

Summer Solstice   Winter Solstice   Winter Solstice   Summer Solstice

2020   15020

Above: A dramatic example highlighting the effects of the earth's wobble. On the left, in the year 2020, the summer solstice took place in the constellation of Gemini and the winter solstice took place in in the constellatio of Sagittarius. However, 12,000 years later in 15020, because of precession, the earth will be tilted in the opposite direction . The winter solstice will happen in in the constellation of Gemini and the summer solstice wil happen in the constellation of Sagittarius.

Winter solstice in 4020 as the sun sets. The zodiac constellations have continued to shift their RA's forward so that the sun now starts to shift out of the constellation of Scorpio. The summer solstice will take place in Taurus and the spring and fall equinoxes in Aquarius and Leo, respectively. A new cosmos has been born.

Part Four

Heavenly Flood

"On earth as in Heaven, As in heaven for as on earth."
– Hermes Trismegistus

Heavenly Waters
Divine Rains – 5500 BCE

The ability of the human imagination to create a narrative from observations of the world around is the underlying process behind any great piece of literature. And it is with the power of our own imaginations that we can understand the ancient mind and witness a narrative unfold in the night skies above southern Iraq in just the same way that the Mesopotamians once did.

Imagine it is the winter solstice in 5500 BCE. As we stand on the shores of the **Euphrates**, looking up at the night sky, we realize it is a special time of the year. Though many Mesopotamian constellations have not yet been created, early Mesopotamians likely recognized patterns of stars in the sky. However, one feature dominates the night sky—the Milky Way, which lies above the southern horizon like a celestial river. Its appearance like this during the rainy season must have been decreed by the gods and must be the source of the divine rains that pour down, bringing life and fertility to the earth below.

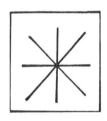

The Sumerian "Engur" sign

Left: This sign was used by the Sumerians to represent the fertile subterranean waters believed to reside beneath the earth. But the sign could also be used by the Sumerians to refer to the celestial heavens. This double meaning of the Engur sign demonstrates how the Mesopotamians connected the celestial heavens with fertile waters. When the ancient Greeks later adopted Mesopotamian astrology, they too associated the southern winter skies with rain, naming them "the waters."

Winter solstice 5500 BCE.
Looking up at the night sky in
southern Iraq at midnight you would
notice the milky way laying across
the southern horizon.

Milky Way

East   South   West

In a period where many constellations were not yet fully developed, the Milky Way was one of
the most impressive sights dominating the night sky. Its appearance across the southern horizon
coincided with the rainy season.

Waters of Chaos
Birth of the Ark – 4800 BCE

During the winter solstice in 4800 BCE a remarkable event has happened—the Milky Way has shifted upward as it "floods" the southern horizon and, in doing so, reveals the first appearance of a new star peeking over the southern horizon. This new star, now known as Canopus, is the second brightest star in the night sky, and it demands the attention of the observers below. Interpreted as a divine approval, it floats just below the Milky Way. However, the arrival of this bright new star, initially, can only be seen from Eridu, the first city in southern Mesopotamia. The new star on the bank of the celestial river (Milky Way) mirrors the city of Eridu on the bank of the Euphrates. As a celestial representation of the earthly city, Canopus will become known as the Star of Eridu. This astounding event will be remembered, and passed orally from generation to generation and, over time, will be a sign from the water god Enki and his fertile flood waters.

Eventually the earthly city of Eridu and the Star of Eridu will become dedicated to Enki—the same god who warns of the Great Flood in the various tales.

Left: The City of Eridu had a special temple dedicated to Enki. It was located on a mound in the middle of a lagoon and represented the moment of creation when the world rose from the waters of chaos; an idea that was later reflected with the symbol of the ark.

60

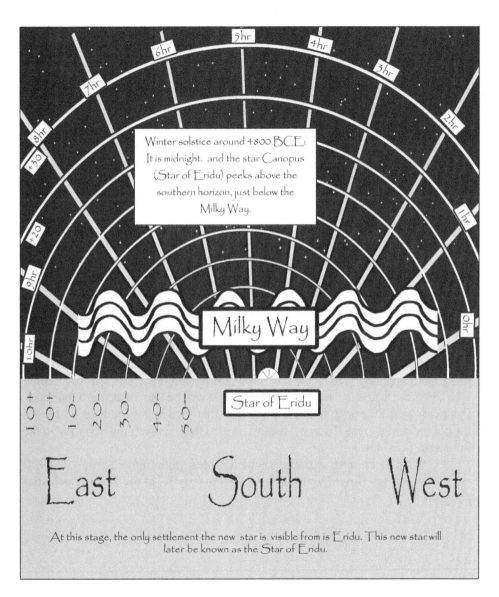

Winter solstice around 4800 BCE: It is midnight, and the star Canopus (Star of Eridu) peeks above the southern horizon, just below the Milky Way.

Milky Way

Star of Eridu

East South West

At this stage, the only settlement the new star is visible from is Eridu. This new star will later be known as the Star of Eridu.

Flooded Skies
A Celestial Warning – 3000 BCE

By 3000 BCE, the star of Eridu has shifted upward so that on the winter solstice at midnight, it is clearly visible across much of Mesopotamia. However, it has also become clear that there has been a cataclysm in the heavens. Because of the earth's precession, the whole sky appears to twist leftward pivoting around a central point—the star of Eridu. As a result, the western part of the Milky Way shifts upward, flooding the western part of the sky. During this "Great Flood," as the sky twists leftward, there are many eastern stars that will never rise on this day again, having been "destroyed" by the descending eastern section of the Milky Way. However, the Star of Eridu is safe as it floats on the horizon. In the western part of the sky the constellation Bull of Heaven, which represents livestock, takes on a more prominent position, having shifted its DEC upward by about 5 degrees as it rises to safety along with its savior the "ark."

For the Mesopotamian mind, these celestial movements were a divine narrative; a message from the cosmos about the interconnected nature of heaven and earth. This idea would have certainly been reinforced by a local but devastating earthly flood that took place in the region around 2900 BCE.

Between the first sighting of the Star of Eridu and now, another strange thing has happened. The winter solstice sun no longer appears in the "Great One" but has shifted to a new constellation that will be known as the "Goatfish." It appears as if the sun god Utu has signaled that the Great Flood has destroyed the old order and created a new cosmos; an idea that parallels the narrative in the Sumerian flood tale.

Soon afterward, expressions of the Mesopotamian cosmic view will start to be written down, veiled behind various myths in the form of celestial allegories.

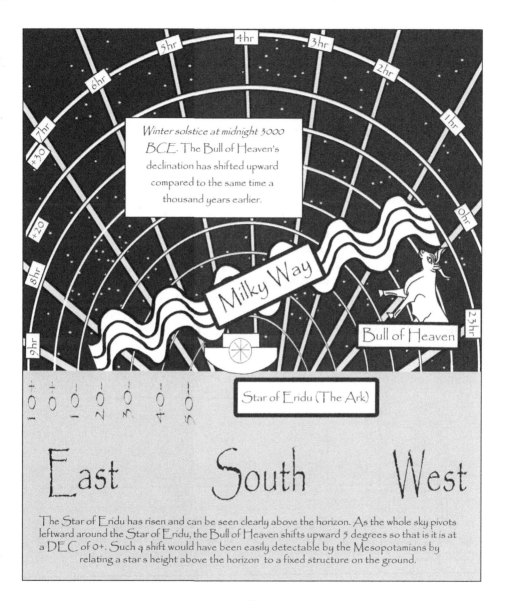

Winter solstice at midnight 3000 BCE. The Bull of Heaven's declination has shifted upward compared to the same time a thousand years earlier.

Milky Way

Bull of Heaven

Star of Eridu (The Ark)

East   South   West

The Star of Eridu has risen and can be seen clearly above the horizon. As the whole sky pivots leftward around the Star of Eridu, the Bull of Heaven shifts upward 5 degrees so that is it is at a DEC of 0+. Such a shift would have been easily detectable by the Mesopotamians by relating a star s height above the horizon to a fixed structure on the ground.

Beasts and Mountains
The Lion and Supa – 3000 – 2000 BCE

Between 3000 and 2000 BCE, it becomes apparent to astrologers that the Great Flood is not yet over. The earth's precession causes the western portion of the Milky Way to continue pivoting around the Star of Eridu, which "appears" to have stopped rising above the horizon and now stands stationary. It has also becomes apparent that the constellation called the Lion, (which represents "wild animals"), has shifted upward along with the Bull of Heaven. For now, it is not just the Bull of Heaven (livestock), that is being saved; it is both domesticated and wild animals. Soon after 2000 BCE, the Akkadian flood tale will start to appear and the narrative will include not just the livestock being saved but also the wild animals.

At the same time, something remarkable is happening in the northeastern part of the sky. Since 4000 BCE one of the most important Mesopotamian constellations, Supa, (below left) rose during the winter solstice before the Star of Eridu. However this constellation has been slowly shifting its RA leftward so that after 2000 BCE, its brightest star, Arcturus, which represents part of the celestial mountain peak, starts to rise after the now stationary Canopus. Soon after this event, we see the addition of the ark coming to rest on a northwestern mountain to the plot of the flood tale.

Above: The star Arcturus was located toward the bottom of the Supa constellation.

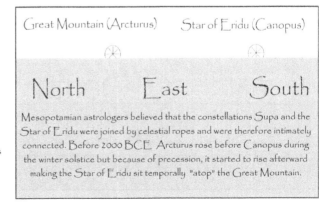

Great Mountain (Arcturus)   Star of Eridu (Canopus)

North   East   South

Mesopotamian astrologers believed that the constellations Supa and the Star of Eridu were joined by celestial ropes and were therefore intimately connected. Before 2000 BCE, Arcturus rose before Canopus during the winter solstice but because of precession, it started to rise afterward making the Star of Eridu sit temporally "atop" the Great Mountain.

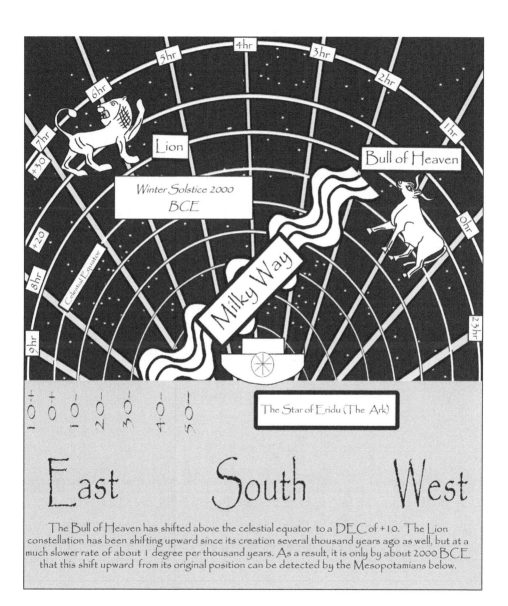

The Bull of Heaven has shifted above the celestial equator to a DEC of +10. The Lion constellation has been shifting upward since its creation several thousand years ago as well, but at a much slower rate of about 1 degree per thousand years. As a result, it is only by about 2000 BCE that this shift upward from its original position can be detected by the Mesopotamians below.

65

Mesopotamian Zodiac
Sublime Echoes

The Mesopotamian zodiac was recognized relatively late in Mesopotamia, probably not until around 1000 BCE, although some constellations that would eventually become part of it, such as the Lion, the Bull of Heaven, and the Scorpion, were likely developed in the 5th and 4th millennia BCE.

Hired Man

Lion

Pabilsag

Bull of Heaven

Furrow and Frond

Goatfish

Great Twins

Scales

Great One

Crab

Scorpion

Anunitum & Swallow

However, the period around 2000 BCE saw the development and formation of a number of newer constellations, including the birds that were taken abord the ark, such as the Raven, Anunitum (the Dove), and the Swallow.

The development of these newer constellations was to have a profound effect on later interpretations of the night sky, as their movements across the heavens would eventually allow for a greater variety of allegorical expression.

Above: By around 1000 BCE, many of the constellations that would eventually form the zodiac circle had been created. Texts such as the Mul.Apin also preserved knowledge of these constellations for future generations of Mesopotamian priests.

The Mesopotamian zodiac circle was
completed by 1000 BCE.

Astral Messengers
Dove, Swallow, and Raven 2000 – 1000 BCE

Since around 2000 BCE, many new constellations have been taking their final form in the night sky. These include those known as the Raven, Anunitum (Dove), and Swallow. However, at this stage, these three constellations all have one thing in common—their different positions in the sky all lie directly over the celestial equator. But things are about to change, and when they do, these constellations will serve as celestial messengers.

As the second millennium BCE progresses, the skies above Mesopotamia continue to twist eastward as they had been doing for thousands of years, shifting the heavens around the Star of Eridu, which continues to appear stationary.

However, by 2000 BCE Ziggurats started appearing across much of Mesopotamia, and with them the organization necessary to measure a star or constellations lateral position. The insights that these new measurements provided allowed greater interpretations of the night sky to be made. In a relatively short space of time, the constellations Anunitum (the Dove) and the Swallow located in the western part of the sky where the Milky Way is the highest above the horizon, move above the celestial equator and shift their RA towards the Star of Eridu.

However, the Raven in the eastern part of the sky is shifting away from the Star of Eridu and its declination has moved below the celestial equator as it descends along with the eastern section of the Milky Way, which has slowly been lowering below the horizon.

Around 1000 BCE, we start to see in the Gilgamesh version of the flood myth, the narrative of the protagonist releasing three birds to determine if the flood is over. The dove and swallow return to the ark (Star of Eridu) but the raven does not, signaling the lowering floodwaters.

Left: Seal impression from Uruk depicting the constellations Swallow and Anunitum joined together by a ribbon-like cord known as the "tails." The association between birds and fish was especially strong in Mesopotamia. Later the Greeks combined Anunitum and the Swallow to create the constellation Pisces.

The Raven shifts its RA from about 8.5 hrs. to 9.5 hrs. as it moves away from the Star of Eridu.

The Dove and Swallow have shifted their RA from 22hrs to 23hrs moving closer to the Star of Eridu.

Bull of Heaven

Lion

Milky Way

Raven

Dove & Swallow

Star of Eridu (The Ark)

East   South   West

Winter Solstice 1000 BCE – In the west, the floodwaters of the Milky Way continue to rise. As it does so, Anunitum (Dove) and Swallow rise above the celestial equator on the flooded side of the sky, shifting its position toward the ark. Meanwhile the Raven is shifting away from the ark as it descends below the celestial equator with the lowering eastern "floodwaters" of the Milky Way

An Eternal Rainbow
The Final Flood 1000 – 600 BCE

It only takes several hundred years for the final development of the flood tale to happen. And in this short amount of time, something astonishing has happened in the skies of the winter solstice. By 1000 BCE, the water constellation called the Rainbow, which sits just above the Dove's head, shifts upward so that it sits on the same declination as the sun at its highest point during the summer months.

The Rainbow constellation has always been a good sign, associated with fertile rains, abundance, and renewal. Its new position on the sacred solstice declination was also viewed positively by the Mesopotamian priests and astrologers.

Also, during this time, the winter solstice sun has been slowly shifting out of the constellation of the Goatfish, signaling the destruction of the old cosmos and the birth of a new one. For now, it is no longer the Raven that signals the flood is over, but the Dove, with the Rainbow positioned directly above. It is as if the gods are promising that this is the last of the great floods and they shall never happen again.

This poetic interpretation coincides with the conclusion of the biblical version of the flood tale, where the returning dove signals the end of the flood and god places a rainbow in the sky signaling his promise to never flood the world again. Along with changes to its cultural narrative, this version will be handed down across the western world when it is included in the Old Testament.

Right: The olive branch was considered a symbol of peace by the ancient Greeks and was adopted by various regions in the eastern Mediterranean. The inclusion of the returning dove carrying an olive branch was a late addition to the biblical flood tale and underlined its authors' interpretation that the cosmic cycle of destruction had come to end.

70

Winter Solstice 700 BCE
The constellation Rainbow
has shifted upwards so that it
lies directly on +23.5 DEC.

East   South   West

The sun sets during the winter solstice. The sun shifting out of the constellation Goatfish
represents the end of an era. The Dove appears directly overhead with the Rainbow having shifted
so that it lays at the same declination of the summer solstice sun. It is as if the heavens are signaling
that the flood is truly over and that the Great Flood will never happen again.

71

Conclusion
Reevaluating History

We now reach one of the most fascinating parts of our journey—putting all the pieces together. We have seen many versions of the flood tale spanning several millennia, showing us how the narrative developed overtime. We also know that many elements of the plot were also constellations. But most exciting of all, we have seen how the development of the flood tale coincided with the creation of those constellations and their movements over long periods.

This begs the question, could the Great Flood tale be an ancient commentary on the effects of the earth's precession on the night sky? The likely possibility that there is a secret code embedded within a piece of literature that has remained hidden from scholars and religion for over 2000 years is more than astonishing.

How are we to understand ancient society considering this new evidence? How was such a prominent aspect of Mesopotamian culture able to transcend and develop in so many regions over several millennia while keeping its secret meaning intact? And what implications does it have for our understanding of how information is disseminated in our own times?

As more Mesopotamian tablets are discovered and translated, we shall no doubt learn more than ever about the origins of the world's first civilizations, and how many of our fundamental assumptions about them are wrong. History may have to be rewritten no matter how uncomfortable it may seem as first. However the reward will be worth it, for not only will we have a much deeper and more realistic understanding of the past, but a clearer understanding of ourselves in the present.

Left: It is said that the ancient Greek astronomer, Hipparchus, discovered the precession of the equinoxes in 127 BCE. However, as we have seen, the ancient Mesopotamians were aware of its presence thousands of years earlier and expressed it through allegory. Our whole understanding of the ancient past begs reexamination.

An 1896 Illustration of the rainbow appearing after the Great Flood, taken from "My Mother's Bible Stories," John H. Vincent, 1896.

The impact of the Great Flood tale across cultures has been tremendous. Perhaps its powerful ability to transcend time and place and capture such a broad audience is that we, as humans, subconsciously recognize that beneath the story's surface lies a hidden truth about the ideas its authors were communicating.

Epilogue
A Lasting Legacy

The impact that Mesopotamian literature, such as the Great Flood tale and the Epic of Gilgamesh, was to have on the western world was immense. Its influence was felt around the ancient Mediterranean for some time, and guided the development of Greek myths, such as the ***Odyssey*** and the ***Labors of Hercules***. In fact, many scholars now believe that several Roman and Greek myths have as their origins the interpretations of celestial observations; a practice in keeping with the Near East.

However, it was not until the conquests of Alexander the Great that Mesopotamian culture was to make its greatest impact. Besides being responsible for the introduction of Mesopotamian astrology to the West, the period also saw the adoption and refinement of the art of communicating ideas through allegory when it later became the foundation of the most esoteric of Arts—***alchemy***. Known as the Royal Art, alchemy has its roots in early ***Hellenic Egypt*** and was influenced by astrology that originated from Mesopotamia. Adopted by the West, it used colorful esoteric metaphors and allegories as a way of disguising its ideas from the uninitiated, a tradition that continued well into the 19th century.

Above: Many Greek myths such as the *Labors of Hercules* were inspired or derived from much older Mesopotamian versions that were based on celestial observations

But perhaps the biggest impact these ancient stories had were of a more universal nature. Whether or not their true meaning was understood, these allegorical tales had the effect of inspiring the ancient imagination and instilling a sense of hope in the ability of the human race to communicate and interact with the universe for the benefit of humankind.

Dance of Death, The Astrologer, Hans Holbein, 1526.

Western alchemy, like Gilgamesh, sought to discover the secret of immortality. The art was influenced by astrology originating from Mesopotamia, and, likewise, communicated ideas and observations in the form of allegory.

75

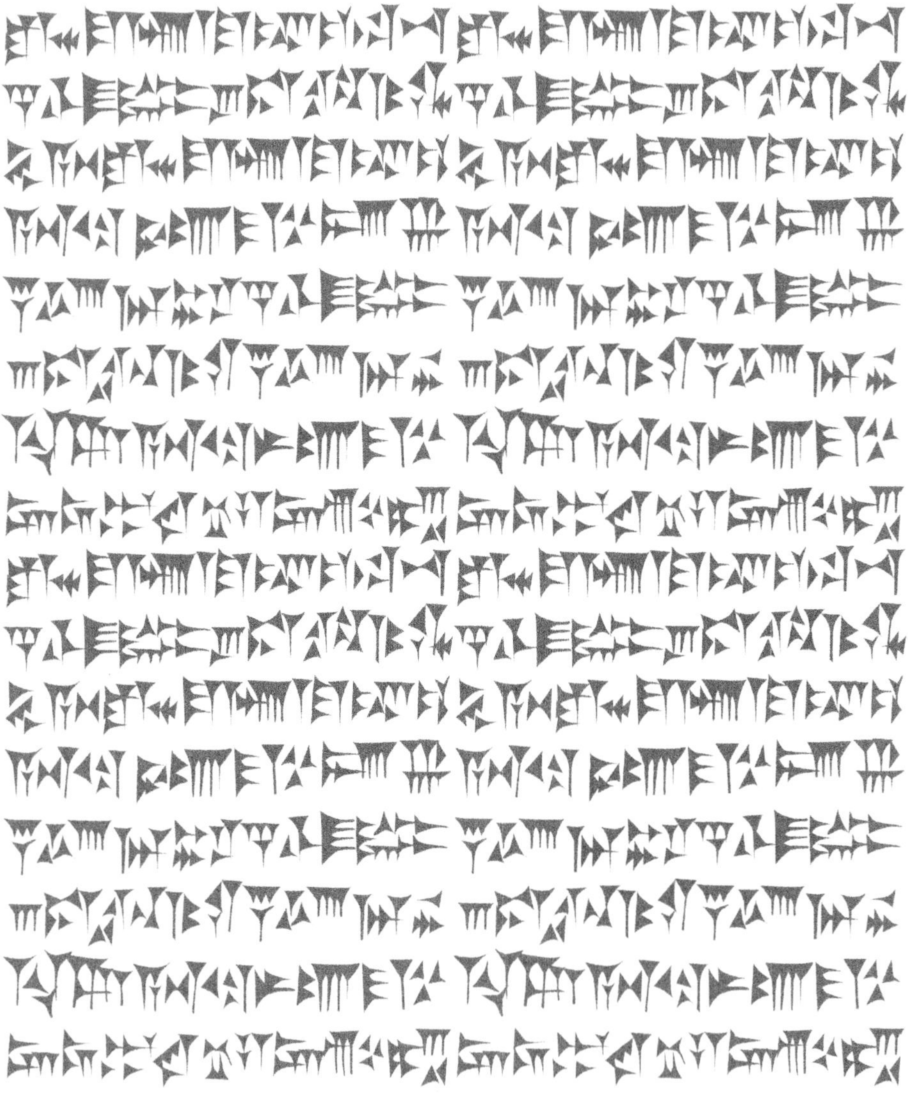

Appendices

Appendix 1: Chronology of Mesopotamian Astrology

All Dates in BCE

35000 Modern humans

Stone Age humans settle in Mesopotamia.

9000 First agriculture

First farming of crops and domestication of animals. Likely development of star identification to help with the sowing and harvesting of crops.

7000–5000 First settlements

First villages and irrigation. Founding of Eridu as a settlement. First depictions of constellations in Mesopotamian artwork.

5000 First city

Eridu develops into the first city. Its creation coincides with the first appearance of the star Canopus on the southern horizon two hundred years later. This new star will be named the Star of Eridu and will be associated with Enki.

3500 First city states

First city States developed in Sumer. Sumerian culture dominates the region. First known depiction of the Bull of Heaven.

3000 *Writing developed*

The first writing developed in the region of Sumer. During the winter solstice the Star of Eridu is now clearly visible above the horizon after having shifted upward along with the constellation of the Bull of Heaven. The Milky Way twists leftward causing its western part to "flood the sky." The first oral tales of the Great Flood likely emerged during this time.

2900 *Local Mesopotamian flood*

Local Flooding devastates the region. This event would have certainly been connected with the astral flooding taking place above by the superstitious Mesopotamians below.

2800–2500 *Gilgamesh Era*

Period during which King Gilgamesh likely existed.

2500 *First literature*

First poems that will become part of the Epic of Gilgamesh written around this time. First written references to constellations in the form of allegory. First written accounts of the flood tale included in the Eridu Genesis likely happen during this period.

2334–2154 *Akkadian Empire*

The Akkadian Empire dominates the region. Akkadians adopt many of the aspects of Sumerian culture and religion.

2000 First ziggurats

First ziggurat temples built around this time. Intense focus on observing and recording celestial observations. Many constellations that would later become part of the zodiac started developing during this period. The northeastern star Arcturus, representing a celestial mountain peak, rises at the same time as the Star of Eridu, which appears to remain stationary. During the following millennia, Arcturus starts to rise after Star of Eridu. Descriptions of the ark coming to rest on a mountain in the northeast appears in the Great Flood tale over the following centuries.

1894–1595 First Babylonian Empire

The Babylonian Empire expands and dominates the region, adopting and developing earlier astronomical culture from the Akkadians and Sumerians The constellations Raven, Anunitum (Dove), and Swallow are developed and begin to shift away and toward the Star of Eridu (Ark), respectively. The appearance of the protagonist of the Great Flood tale releasing the Raven, Dove, and Swallow begin to appear shortly after this.

911 Neo-Assyrian Empire

Rise of the Assyrian Empire. Within a couple centuries, Assyria will dominate Mesopotamia. The Assyrians will also inherit the astronomical traditions of the region. Around this time the Rainbow constellation starts to shift upward so that it will eventually lay on the summer solstice declination. Over the next several centuries, the winter solstice sun starts shifting out of the constellation Goatfish signaling the end of the old world and the start of a new era.

625 Second Babylonian Empire

Establishment of the Second Babylonian Empire.

605–518 Babylon conquers the Assyrians, Egyptians, and the Levant

Scholars from the conquered regions brought to Babylon to work in the libraries, where they will be exposed to Mesopotamian literature. The biblical narrative of the Dove returning to the ark signaling the end of the flood, and the Rainbow symbolizing God's promise never to flood the world appears in the Great Flood tale shortly after.

539 Persia invades Mesopotamia

Exiled scholars in Babylon return to their homelands, spreading the Biblical version of the Great Flood tale across neighboring regions.

334 Greeks invade Mesopotamia

Alexandra the Great invades Mesopotamia. Greeks adopt Mesopotamian astronomy and spread it throughout the Mediterranean.

Appendix 2: Empire of Alexander the Great

Alexander the Great's Empire was one of the largest in the ancient world, stretching from Greece in Europe, Egypt in North Africa, and northwestern India in the East. The Empire was instrumental in disseminating Mesopotamian astrology throughout the conquered regions. Ancient Greek and Egyptian astrological records after this conquest reflect Mesopotamian astronomy and can be used to enhance our understanding of how the Mesopotamians saw the night sky.

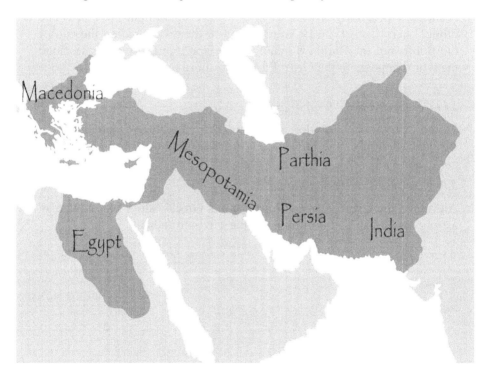

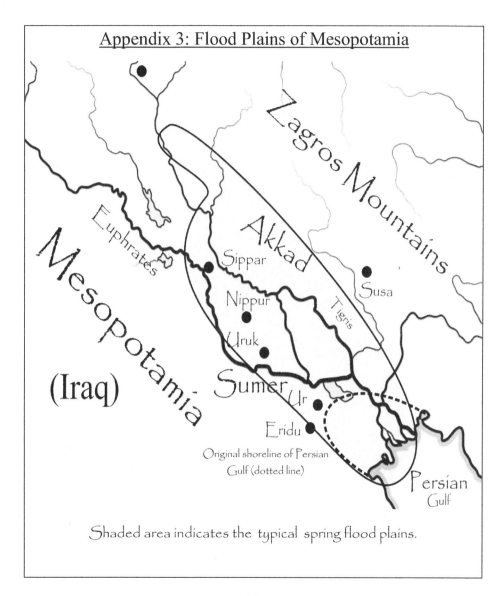

Appendix 3: Flood Plains of Mesopotamia

Shaded area indicates the typical spring flood plains.

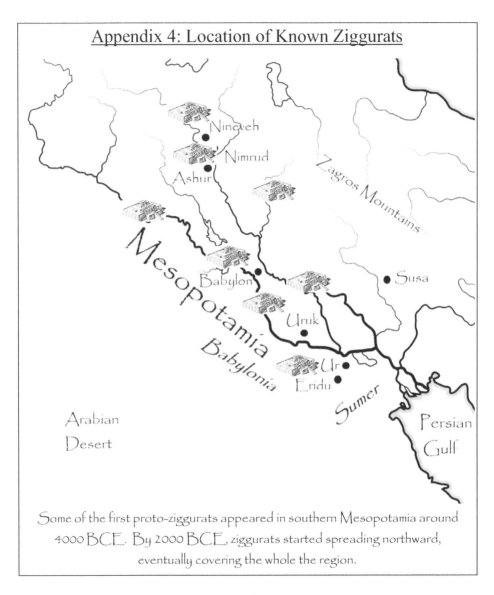

Appendix 4: Location of Known Ziggurats

Nineveh

Nimrud

Ashur

Zagros Mountains

Mesopotamia

Babylon

Susa

Babylonia

Uruk

Ur

Eridu

Sumer

Arabian

Desert

Persian

Gulf

Some of the first proto-ziggurats appeared in southern Mesopotamia around 4000 BCE. By 2000 BCE, ziggurats started spreading northward, eventually covering the whole the region.

Appendix 5: List of Mesopotamian Flood Tablets

List of known Mesopotamian flood story clay tablets discovered so far.

Sumerian Flood Tale Tablets

Old Babylonian Sumerian Schøyen

Sumerian

Akkadian Flood Tale Tablets

Old Babylonian Recession Larsa

Old Babylonian Recession Nippur C_1

Old Babylonian Recession Nippar C_2

Middle Babylonian Ark

Middle Babylonian Ugarit I

Middle Babylonian Ugarit I_1

Middle Babylonian Ugarit I_2

Middle Babylonian Nippur

Middle Babylonian Hattsua

Middle Babylonian Nippur

Neo-Assyrian Nineveh R

Neo-Assyrian Nineveh U

Neo-Assyrian Nineveh W

Neo-Assyrian Nineveh W_1

Assyrian Flood Tale Tablets

Gilgamesh Flood Tablet

Mesopotamian Periods

Old Babylonian 1900–1600 BCE

Middle Babylonian 1600–1200 BCE

Neo-Assyrian 911–609 BCE

Neo-Babylonian 626–539 BCE

---

*For translations of the Akkadian and Gilgamesh Flood tablets see Wasserman, N. *The Flood: The Akkadian Sources Posted at the Zurich Open Repository and Archive.* Zurich: University of Zurich, 2020.

Appendix 6: The Mul.Apin Text

Written between 800–700 BCE, the Mul.Apin is a Babylonian text that provides a catalog of celestial observations that were originally made around 1100 BCE. The text includes a list of 66 stars and constellations, and provides the rising, setting, and culmination dates for many of them. Composed of two tablets, it is one of the most important texts in helping us understand how the Mesopotamians saw the night sky.

The first tablet is the most important and contains the names of constellations, as well as their positions in relation to one another in the following format:

- 33 stars or constellations in the northern part of the sky (called the path of Enlil).
- 23 stars or constellations in the equatorial part of the sky (called the path of Anu).
- 15 stars or constellations in the southern part of the sky (called the path of Ea).

In addition, the first tablet also includes:

- Heliacal rising dates of 34 stars and constellations.
- The number of days between the risings of various stars and constellations.
- The stars and constellations that rise and appear in the night sky at the same time.
- The constellations in the path of moon. As the moon's path is close to the sun's path, it includes all predecessors to the zodiac constellations.

The second tablet provides information regarding making celestial observations. It includes:

- Name's of the planets and their paths across the sky.
- Which stars mark the solstices and equinoxes.
- Instructions for observing the appearances of certain stars.
- How many days each planet is visible during its cycle.
- The stars associated with the four winds.
- The dates when the sun's path is in one of the three celestial paths.
- The duration of days and nights at the solstices and equinoxes and how they are measured.
- Example of celestial omens.

Text of the Mul.Apin

The following is text from the Mul.Apin describing the constellations and their position in relation to each other. (Their position to modern constellations is in brackets.) Reproduced, with kind permission of Gavin White, from *Babylonian Star-Lore*, Solaria Publications.

33 Northern stars on the path of Enlil:

The Plough, Enlil, the lead star of the stars of Enlil (*most of Draco*)

The Wolf at the seed funnel of the Plough (*head & middle of Draco*)

The Old Man, Enmesharra (*Perseus*)

The Crook, the Crouching God (*Auriga*)

The Great Twins, Lugalirra and Meslamtaea (*Gemini*)

The Little Twins, Alammush and Ninezengud (*Canis Minor*)

The Crab, the Seat of Anu (*Cancer*)

The Lion, Latarak (*Leo*)

The stars that stand in the breast of the Lion, the King Star (*the star Regulus in Leo*)

The dusky stars that stand in the tail of the Lion, the Frond of Erua, Zarpanitu (*Coma Berenices & the western part of Virgo*)

Supa, Enlil, who decrees the fate of the land (*Bootes*)

The star before him, the Star of Abundance, the messenger of Ninlil (*a star in the western part of Bootes*)

The star behind him, the Star of Dignity, the messenger of Tishpak (*a star in the eastern part of Bootes*)

The Wagon, Ninlil (*The seven principal stars of Ursa Major*)

The star at the shaft of the Wagon, the Fox, Erra, the strong one among the gods (*the star Zeta in Ursa Major*)

The star at the front of the Wagon, the Ewe, Aya (*probably the star Epsilon in Ursa Major*)

The Hitched Yoke, Anu, the great one of the heavens (*the star Eta in Ursa Major*)

The Wagon of Heaven, Damkianna (*Ursa Minor*)

The star on its rope, the Heir of the Sublime Temple, the first ranking son of Anu (*the star Polaris in Ursa Minor*)

The Standing Gods of the E-kur, the Sitting Gods of the E-kur* (*the western part of Ophiuchus; Corona Borealis*) ***Authors note: E-kur is Sumerian for mountain house. The constellations of the Standing Gods and the Sitting Gods are represented as placed on the slopes of the celestial mountain whose peak is in the constellation Supa.**

The She-Goat, Gula (*Lyra*)

The star before the She-Goat, the Sitting Dog (*most of Hercules*)

The bright star of the She-Goat, Lamma, the messenger of Baba (*the star Vega in Lyra*)

Two stars behind her, Ninsar and Erragal (*the stars Beta and Gamma in Lyra*)

The Panther, Nergal (*most of Cygnus and probably part of Cepheus*)

The star to his right, the Swine, Damu (*probably Delphinus*)

The star to his left, the Horse (*front legs of Pegasus and Lacerta*)

The star behind him, the Stag, messenger of the Star Cluster (*Cassiopeia and part of Andromeda*)

The dusky stars at the breast of the Stag, Harriru, god of the Rainbow (*the spiral galaxy M31 in Andromeda*)

The bright red star at the kidney of the Stag, the Destroyer (*The star Gamma in Cassiopeia*)

23 Equatorial stars on the Path of Anu:

The Field, the seat of Ea, which leads the stars of Anu (the four stars of the Square of Pegasus)

The star at the Field, the Swallow (*the head and neck of Pegasus, the western fish of Pisces*)

The star behind the Field, Anunitum (*the northern fish of Pisces*)

The star behind it, the Hired Man, Dumuzi (*Aries*)

The Star Cluster, the Seven Gods, the Great Gods (*the Pleiades*)

The Bull of Heaven, the Bull's Jaw, the Crown of Anu (*Taurus, or at least its head*)

The True Shepherd of Anu, Papsukal, the messenger of Anu and Ishtar (*Orion*)

The Twins who are opposite the True Shepherd of Anu, Lulal and Latarak (*Cetus and part of Eridanus*)

The star behind him, the Rooster (*Lepus*)

The Arrow, the Arrow of the Great God Ninurta (*the star Sirius and probably other stars in Canis Major*)

The <u>Bow</u>, the Elamite Ishtar, the daughter of Anu (*Puppis*)

The <u>Serpent</u>, Ningishzida, Lord of the Underworld (*Hydra*)

The <u>Raven</u>, the Star of Adad (*Corvus*)

The <u>Furrow</u>, Shala with her ear of barley (*the eastern part of Virgo*)

The <u>Scales</u>, the Horn of the Scorpion (*Libra*)

<u>Zababa</u> (*the eastern part of Ophiuchus*), the <u>Eagle</u> (*Aquila*) and the <u>Dead Man</u> (*Sagitta*)

15 Southern stars on the Path of Ea:

The <u>Fish</u>, Ea, the lead star of the stars of Ea (*Pisces Austrinus*)

The <u>Great One</u>, Ea (*Aquarius*).

The <u>Star of Eridu</u>, Ea* (*Vela*) ***Authors note. The star of Eridu actually forms the stern of the constellation Argo Navis.**

The star to his right, <u>Ninmah</u> (*Vela*)

The <u>Wild Boar</u>, Ningirsu (*most of Centaurus*)

The star to its side, the <u>Harrow</u>, the weapon of Mar-biti, within which one sees the Abyss (*the western part of Centaurus*)

The two stars that are behind him, <u>Shullat and Hanish</u>, Shamas and Adad (*two stars in Centaurus*)

The star behind them, rises like Ea and sets like Ea, Numushda, Adad (*unknown, possibly part of the Milky Way*)

The star to the left of the Scorpion, the Mad Dog, Kusu (*Lupus*)

The Scorpion, Ishhara, the Governess of the Lands (*Scorpio*)

The Breast of the Scorpion, Lisi and Nabu (*The star Antares in Scorpio*)

The two stars on the Stinger of the Scorpion, Sharur and Shargaz (*the stars Lambda and Nu in Scorpio*)

The star behind them, Pabilsag (*Sagittarius*)

The Cargo-Boat (*Corona Australis*) and the Goatfish (*Capricorn*)

Appendix 7: Mesopotamian Astronomical Texts

Throughout Mesopotamian history, it was likely that thousands of astronomical texts recording millennia's worth of observations were made. Unfortunately, most of these records did not survive or are yet to be discovered. The following, however, is a selection of texts that we do have. They cover a range of subjects and periods and are useful in showing us how astronomy developed throughout Mesopotamian history. They also provide us with additional information to the Mul.Apin, which helps us to piece together Mesopotamian constellations and their locations in the night sky.

Enuma And Enlil (EAE) 1595–1157 BCE

An important series of 70 clay tablets composed in the second millennium BCE that list around 7,000 celestial divinations. The first 50 tablets describe how to interpret the appearance of the moon, its position in the sky, lunar eclipses, the sun, clouds, and the weather phenomena. The last 20 tablets deal with divining the planets and stars through the use of using metaphor and allegory.

Many interesting examples of Mesopotamian Omens and their various forms can be found at the University of Pennsylvania's online database at: http: //oracc.museum.upenn.edu /saao/ saa08/corpus

The EAE Commentaries

The following are a class of Mesopotamian texts whose purpose was to provide clarification to court astrologers attempting to interpret the EAE.

Mukallimtu Commentaries

Parts of these texts helped explain the allegorical parts of astrological omens in EAE by clarifying certain words and shedding light on their true meaning.

Satu

Satu provided a linguistic commentary of the EAE. It explained various astrological meanings and correct pronunciation of certain symbols and words contained in some omens.

Summa Sin Ina Tamarti-Su

This text provided a full astrological and linguistic commentary on the EAE. Not only did it explain the various meanings of certain words and how to pronounce them, but it also told the astrologer how to interpret the various allegories.

Astrological Texts

Great Star List

A star list that includes names of planets, constellations, and group of stars. There is also a section with information on the months and the division of the night watches.

Gudea Inscriptions 2000 BCE

Inscriptions written about 2000 BCE. Among other things, they provide a glimpse into the early astrology and symbolism of Mesopotamia, lending to our understanding of the development of constellations.

The Gu-text 700–500 BCE

The Gu-text lists the stars in the night sky running from north to south and provides valuable information in locating the positions of Mesopotamian constellations. Although this text was written between the 7th and 5th centuries BCE, it is believed to be compiled from a much older source.

Old Babylonian Star Lists 2000–1600 BCE

These are several separate texts that list the names of Mesopotamian constellations. They include a text known as the Nippur Forerunner written around 2000 BCE. Its origins are likely much older, having been written in the Sumerian language. It lists many of the constellations that can be found in the Mul.Apin. This indicates the accurate continuity of constellations throughout Mesopotamian history.

VR 46 600–500 BCE

A star list from the late Babylonian period. The text lists stars and constellations and their qualities through epithets.

Weidner Star-Text 800–700 BCE

A brief Assyrian text that describes many of Mesopotamian constellations.

Astrolabes 1900 BCE

The Astrolabes (not to be confused with astronomical measuring devices) are some of the earliest texts on astronomy. Astrolabes are lists of stars that are often set out in the form of three concentric circles. Though not star charts in the traditional sense, they can provide a valuable reference for our understanding of the evolution of Mesopotamian astronomy.

Appendix 8: Mesopotamian Star Chart 1100 BCE

Reconstruction of the Mesopotamian constellations. Taken from *Babylonian Star-Lore: An Illustrated Guide to the Star-Lore and Constellations of Ancient Babylonia*, Gavin White, Solaria Publications, 2014.

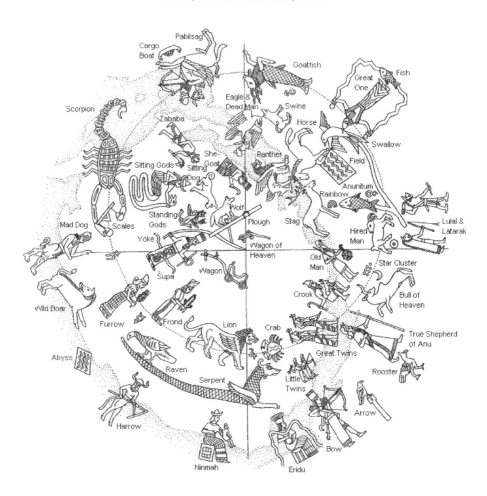

Appendix 9: Ancient Greek Star Chart 200 BCE

Reconstruction of the ancient Greek constellations using medieval Arabic sources. Taken from *Babylonian Star-Lore: An Illustrated Guide to the Star-Lore and Constellations of Ancient Babylonia*, Gavin White, Solaria Publications, 2014. Many Mesopotamian constellations were Hellenized after being adopted by the Greeks in order to provide a familiar cultural context. However, the underlying symbolism often remained similar. Notice that the star of Eridu (Canopus), which represented the ark, has now been transformed into part of a larger constellation represented by the ship Argo.

Appendix 10: Ancient Egyptian Star Chart – 30 BCE

The Dendera Zodiac from the Egyptian Dendera temple complex (30 BCE) was heavily influenced by Mesopotamian astrology, which was imported after the conquest of Egypt by Alexander the Great. It contains a great number of the constellations mentioned in the Mul.Apin represented in traditional Egyptian style. Circled is the Star of Eridu, represented by an Egyptian goddess holding jars from which pour the celestial flood waters.

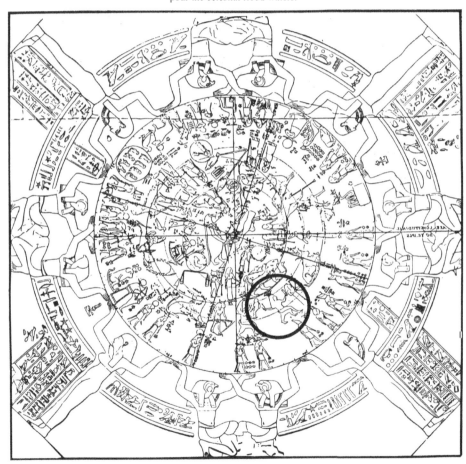

Appendix 11: Farnese Atlas – Second Century CE

Left: The Farnese Atlas is a second century Roman copy of a Greek statue of Atlas holding the celestial sphere showing the constellations. Greek constellations, which were derived from Mesopotamian astrology, were later adopted by the Romans.

Below: A star chart based on the constellations of the Farnese Atlas. It contains all the "traditional" western constellations that we are familiar with today. The Romans were responsible for the final development of the Greek constellations and their spread across Western Europe.

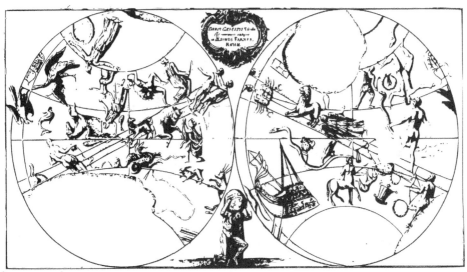

Appendix 12: Jewish Zodiac – Sixth Century CE

This depiction of the Zodiac is from a sixth-century synagogue in Beit Alpha, Israel. It depicts Greek constellations that were derived from Mesopotamia, showing us the importance of astrology in ancient religions across the region.

Appendix 13: Evolution of the Zodiac

The constellations that make up the western zodiac have their origins in Mesopotamia. They remained surprisingly constant throughout the millennia and underwent only minor changes as they were adopted by the Ancient Greeks, Romans, and modern civilizations.

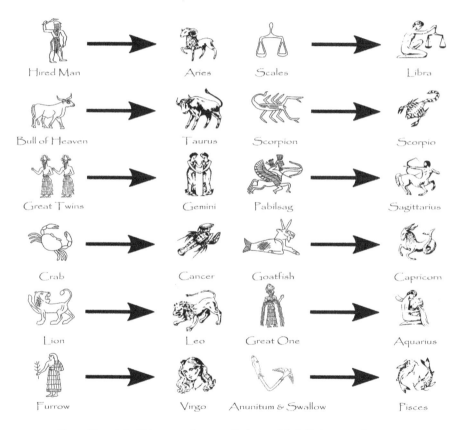

Above: The original Mesopotamian constellations and their final western form thousands of years later.

Appendix 14: Western Traditional Star Chart

Old sky map depicting constellations and zodiac signs of the Northern and Southern Hemispheres. Traditional western constellations were inherited from the Romans but many can trace their origins back to Mesopotamia. Created by Frederick De Wit, Amsterdam, 1680.

Northern Hemisphere

Southern Hemisphere

Appendix 15 Modern Star Chart – 1922 CE

The modern constellations in use today were adopted in 1922. Although they are based on traditional constellations, there are some differences. For example, the constellation Argo Navis was broken up into three separate constellations called Puppis, Carina, and Vega. Modern constellations are depicted in a rather more prosaic style then their predecessors as simple lines connecting the stars that compose the constellation.

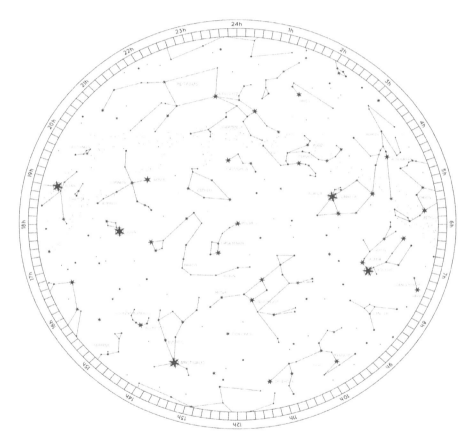

Northern Hemisphere

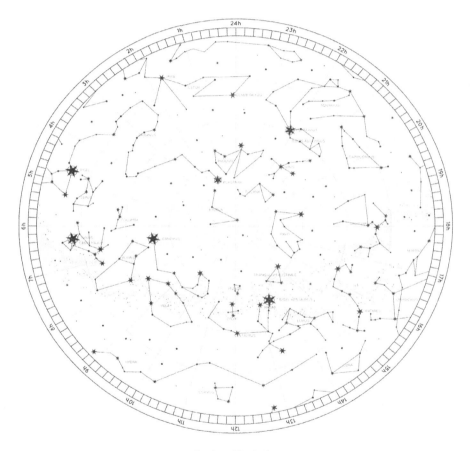

Southern Hemisphere

105

Glossary

Adad: Akkadian name for a storm and rain god originating from northern Mesopotamia and southern Levant. Adad was also identified as a storm god called Ba'al by the Canaanites.

Akitu: Mesopotamian festival celebrated around the time of the spring equinox, which marked the resetting of the solar calendar. Taking place over 12 days, it was practiced across the various cultures of Mesopotamia. In Babylonia, it was later dedicated to Marduk's triumph over Tiamat.

Akkadian: Extinct Mesopotamian language that was used throughout the region by various cultures, including the Akkadian Empire, Old Assyrian Empire, Babylonian Empire, and later, the Middle Assyrian Empire. Most of the Great Flood tales that survived were written using this language.

alchemy: The attempt to purify base metals into gold, and the creation of an elixir of immortality. The practice originated in Hellenic Egypt and drew upon Greek, Egyptian, and Mesopotamian philosophy and astrology. It was later adopted by the West where it was developed and practiced up until the 19th century.

Alexander the Great: Ancient Macedonian king who conquered the Levant, Syria, and Egypt in 332 BCE, Mesopotamia in 331 BCE, and Persia in 330 BCE. At the time, Alexander's empire was the largest that had ever existed and stretched all the way to India. It was responsible for the infusion of Mesopotamian astronomy into the West.

Argo Navis: A large Greek constellation in the southern sky that included the star Canopus (Star of Eridu). It was named after the *Argo*, the mythical ship that took Jason and the Argonauts to Colchis in search of the Golden Fleece. The interpretation of this constellation as a ship was influenced by Mesopotamian astrology, which associated this part of the sky with storms and ships through the star Canopus.

ark: Large wooden ship built by the protagonists to protect their family and animals from the Great Flood. Some of the first ships created by humankind are believed to have originated in Mesopotamia.

Ashurbanipal: King of the Neo-Assyrian Empire between 668–631 BCE. He is credited with creating the first organized library in the world at his capital Nineveh, containing over 30,000 clay tablets representing a broad collection of genres.

Atra-Hasis: Protagonist of the Atra-Hasis Epic. Atra-Hasis means "exceedingly wise" and according to some sources, he was the king of a city called Shuruppak.

Atra-Hasis Epic: Akkadian text describing the creation of the world. The text also includes the Akkadian version of the flood tale.

clay tablet: A writing medium used throughout Mesopotamia. Wedge like markings, called cuneiform, were pressed onto wet clay tablets using reed pens, and be left to dry in the sun. Clay tablets were one of the earliest mediums of writing, having been used since 3000 BCE.

constellation: A group of visible stars that are visualized as an object, often as characters from religious myth. Constellations are some of the world's earliest art forms with some examples dating back to 17,000 BCE.

documentary hypothesis: A hypothesis that the first five books of the Bible, Genesis (which includes the biblical flood story), Exodus, Leviticus, Numbers, and Deuteronomy, are made up from many sources and different authors over several centuries.

Dumuzi: Ancient Mesopotamian god of vegetation and the goddess Inanna's consort. In the myth of Inanna's descent to the underworld, Inanna decreed that Dumuzi was to spend half the year in the underworld and half the year with her. The myth was used to explain the cause of the seasons and heavily influenced the development of the Greek myth of Hades and Persephone.

EA: Akkadian name for Enki.

Enki: Sumerian god of water. He was the god that warned the protagonist in the Mesopotamian flood tales of the coming flood and gave instructions to build an ark. He was depicted as a man holding an overflowing vase, which represented the celestial floodwaters pouring down to Earth. Enki was the patron god of Eridu and was associated with the Star of Eridu and the constellation known as a the "Great One," which was depicted similarly as a man holding an overflowing jar.

Enlil: Chief god of the Sumerian Pantheon. He was adopted by the Akkadians, Babylonians, and Assyrians and was associated with wind, air, and storms. His main temple was in Nippur and was believed to be the mooring rope between heaven and earth. In the Akkadian versions of the flood tale, Enlil was the god responsible for causing the Great Flood. One of his titles was the Great Mountain and he was associated with the constellation Supa, which was believed to sit atop a great celestial mountain.

The constellation was later associated with mountains when the Greeks associated it with Arcas, a mythical Greek hero who was said to have lived in the mountains of Arcadia. The tradition of associating this part of the sky with mountains continued when Johannes Hevelius (1678), influenced by this Greek myth created a new constellation called Mount Maenalus in exactly the same location as the ancient celestial peak.

Epic of Gilgamesh: Originally five independent poems about Gilgamesh the king of UR (2700 BCE). Later these poems were integrated into a single, larger epic recounting the story of Gilgamesh's quest for immortality. Later additions to the epic included the story of Utnapishtim and the Great Flood.

Equator: Imaginary line encircling the earth perpendicular to its axis of rotation dividing the Northern and Southern Hemispheres.

Eridu: Ancient Sumerian city located in southern Sumer, near the shores of the Euphrates River. The Sumerians believed it was the first city in the world. Archeological research indicates that a city existed there since at least 5000 BCE. Originally, Eridu was a fishing city close to the Persian coast but silting of the Euphrates estuary over the following 1000 years shifted the coast so that it currently lies over 100 miles to the east. Eridu was also thought to be the home to Enki, and the city's temple was dedicated to him.

Eridu Genesis: Sumerian story that describes the creation of the world, humans, and the founding of the first cities and the Sumerian flood tale. It is believed to have been composed between 3000–2500 BCE although some parts of it may be older having been passed down orally.

Euphrates: One of the longest rivers in western Asia. Running through Mesopotamia, the Euphrates originates in Armenia and runs southward across the length of Iraq to empty in the Persian Gulf. The river was important as a trade route and, along with the Tigris, was the source of the spring floods that provided fertile material, making the first agricultural settlements possible.

Genesis: The first book in the Hebrew Bible and the Christian Old Testament. The Book of Genesis includes the story of Noah's Ark and the Great Flood.

Gilgamesh: Protagonist of the Epic of Gilgamesh. He was said to be three-quarters human and one-quarter god. Most scholars believe that Gilgamesh was based on a historical king of the Sumerian city-state Uruk sometime between 2800 and 2500 BCE.

Great One: The name of a Mesopotamian constellation. The Great One is a precursor to the modern constellation, Aquarius. It is an incredibly old constellation, dating back to nearly 5000 BCE. The constellation was depicted similarly to Enki as a man holding an overflowing vase representing the celestial rains.

Harriru: Mesopotamian god associated with the rainbow. He represented the fertile rains of the rainy season. The appearance of a rainbow after a storm was viewed as a positive sign from the gods.

Hellenic Egypt: Period when Egypt was ruled by Hellenic (Greek) rulers. It started in 305 BCE with Ptolemy I Sote and ended in 30 BCE with the death of Cleopatra.

Inanna: Sumerian god of fertility, sex, and war, and wife of Dumuzi. She was known as Ishtar by the Akkadians, Babylonians, and Assyrians. She represented the planet Venus and was associated with the constellation Anunitum. (Anunitum translates to "goddess of heaven," a title given to Inanna.) She is often represented in the form of a Dove.

So strong was the connection between Venus, fish, and doves in the region that in nearby Syria, the local goddess who represented Venus, Atargatis, was said to have been hatched from an egg that was that was rolled out of the Euphrates by a fish and brooded by a dove.

kidney: The Mesopotamians knew that the kidney was associated with the creation of urine and the act of urination. It was therefore associated with the Star of Eridu and the Great One as a metaphor of the celestial waters pouring from Heaven.

Labors of Hercules: Myth about a Greek hero called Hercules who must undertake 12 tasks as penance for killing his wife in a fit of madness. It is widely accepted that the Labors of Hercules was influenced by a much older Mesopotamian myth (the myth of the Slain Heroes) that had its roots in the precession of archaic Mesopotamian constellations.

meridian: An imaginary line that runs from the North Pole to the South Pole. Every point of earth lies under a meridian line and is analogous to longitude.

Mesopotamia: The word Mesopotamia is Greek for "between the two rivers." This is a reference to the area between the Euphrates and Tigris rivers that enclose what is present day Iraq. This area saw the development of the first cities, and inventions such as the wheel, agriculture, irrigation, domestication of animals, and written language.

metonymy: The substitution of an object's name with something that it is associated with. An example would be referring to the president and his staff as the "White House" (e.g., "the White House had no comment on the situation").

Mt. Ararat: Mountain in the far east of Turkey. Its location was northeast in relation to the location of the biblical flood story's setting.

Mt. Nisir: A mountain in northeast Iraqi Kurdistan. Its location was northeast in relation to the location of the biblical flood story's setting.

Mul.Apin: See Appendix 6, p. 86.

mundane astrology: The practice of astrology that attempts to predict world or national events. It is distinct from personal astrology, which focuses on predicting events surrounding an individual.

Neo-Babylonian Empire: Second Babylonian Empire lasting from 626–539 BCE, after which it was destroyed by the Persians. At its height, it encompassed the whole of Mesopotamia and the Levant. The Neo-Babylonian Empire was responsible for displacing many peoples from conquered territories by bringing them to Babylonia, an event recorded in the bible as the exile.

Neolithic: A period of prehistory in the near east from 12,000 to 6,500 years ago. It saw the development of the first agriculture and was followed by the development of metallurgy preceding the Bronze Age.

Nineveh: An ancient city in northern Assyria that was the capital of the Neo-Assyrian Empire. Located on the banks of the River Tigris, it was briefly the world's largest city during the seventh century BCE and was home to the Library of Ashurbanipal.

Nippur: Ancient Sumerian city located in northern Sumer. It was an important city being the seat of the Sumerian god ***Enlil*** and believed to be a "mooring rope" between heaven and Earth.

Odyssey: Ancient Greek tale that is one of the earliest texts in the modern Western canon. Composed in the eighth century BCE, it tells the story of Odysseus the King of Ithaca's, ten-year journey home after the Trojan War. The story is believed to be influence by earlier Mesopotamian texts, such as the Epic of Gilgamesh.

omen texts: A class of Mesopotamian texts that attempted to correlate varying observations in nature with specific events taking place on earth.

orbital plane: The plane of the earth's circular orbit around the sun.

Sippar: Ancient Sumerian city located on the east bank of the Euphrates. The city was home to the Sumerian sun god Utu.

Tanakh: The canonical collection of Hebrew scriptures that forms the Hebrew Bible. It includes the Torah, which includes the story of Noah's Ark.

Tiamat: In Babylonia, Tiamat was the primordial goddess of the ocean. She was often portrayed as a sea serpent or dragon. In Mesopotamian myth, she was slain by the god Marduk and her body split into two, creating Earth and the heavens with her tail becoming the Milky Way.

traditional constellations: Classical Western constellations, many of which are still in use today. They were introduced to Europe by the ancient Greeks who adopted and reinterpreted them from the ancient Mesopotamians.

Utnapishtim: Hero of the Babylonian flood tale. Unlike Ziusudra, he was not a king but an ordinary person, although it was said that he was an ancestor of Gilgamesh. He was made immortal for "preserving the seed of life."

Utu: Early Sumerian sun god. He was the twin brother of the goddess Inanna. He was later called Shamash by the Akkadians and came to represent the god of justice. His main temples were in the city of Sippar and Lagash.

Ugarit: Ancient city in northwest Syria. Its location on the coast made it an important gateway city for trade in the Mediterranean. During its history, it was dominated by several empires and absorbed a variety of cultural influences including the flood story.

Ziusudra: Protagonist of the Sumerian flood tale. His name appears in one version of a Sumerian king list, indicating that he was the last king of the Sumerian city Shuruppak before the Great Flood. Scholars believe that Ziusudra was a historical figure who lived around 2900 BCE.

zodiac: Collection of constellations that lay on the ecliptic, which is the path that the sun appears to cross the sky throughout the course of a year.

Bibliography

Alster, B. *Wisdom of Ancient Sumer*. Bethesda: CDL Press, 2005.

Anderson, W.S. *Solving the Mystery of the Biblical Flood*. Bloomington: Xlibris, 2001.

Bailey, L.R. *Noah: The Person and the Story in History and Tradition*. Columbia: University of South Carolina Press, 1989.

Barentine, J.C. *History of Obsolete, Extinct, or Forgotten Star Lore*. New York: Springer, 2015.

Barton, T. *Ancient Astrology*. Abingdon, Oxfordshire: Routledge, 1994.

Best, R.M. *Noah's Ark and the Ziusudra Epic*. University Park, PA: Eisenbrauns, 1999.

Black, Cunningham, Robson, Zolyomi. *The Literature of Ancient Sumer*. Oxford: Oxford University Press, 2004.

Black, J. and Green, A. *Gods, Demons and Symbols of Ancient Mesopotamia*. London: British Museum Press, 1992.

Bottero, J. Mesopotamia: *Writing, Reasoning, and the Gods*. Chicago: University of Chicago Press, 1992.

Botterweck, Johannes; Ringgren, Helmer. *Theological Dictionary of the Old Testament*, Vol 1., Grand Rapids, MI: Wm. B. Eerdmans Publishing Company, 1990.

Bradt, H. *Astronomy Methods*. Cambridge: Cambridge University Press, 2007.

Bunson, A. *Dictionary of Ancient Egypt*. Oxford: Oxford University Press, 1995.

Chen, Y.S. *The Primeval Flood Catastrophe: Origins and Early Development in Mesopotamian Traditions*. Oxford: Oxford University Press, 2013.

115

Roth, Martha T. *Chicago Assyrian Dictionary*. Chicago: Chicago University Press.

Cohen, M. *The Cultic Calendars of the Ancient Near East*. Bethesda: CDL Press, 1993.

Cohn, N. *Noah's Flood: The Genesis Story in Western Thought*. New Haven, CT: Yale University Press, 1996.

Collon, D. *First Impressions*. London: British Museum Press, 1987.

Condos, T. *Star Myths of the Greeks and Romans: A Source Book*. Grand Rapids, MI: Phanes Press, 1997.

Crawford, H. *Sumer and the Sumerians*. Cambridge: Cambridge University Press, 1991.

Crouse, B., and Franz G. "Mount Cudi - The True Mountain of Noah's Ark" Bible and Spade, 19:4, Fall 2006.

Dalley S. *Myths from Mesopotamia*. Oxford: Oxford University press, 1989.

Damrosch, D. *The Buried Book: The Loss and Rediscovery of the Great Epic of Gilgamesh. New York: Henry Holt & Co, 2006.*

De Mieroop, M.V. *History of the Near East*. Oxford: Blackwell Publishing, 2004.

Dundes, A., *The Flood Myth*. Berkeley: University of California Press, 1988.

Eratosthenes, Hyginus. *Constellation Myths: With Aratus's Phaenomena.* Oxford: Oxford World's Classic, 2015.

Enenuru (enenuru.net). Website of online resources for Mesopotamian Studies.

ETCSL (Electronic Text Corpus of Sumerian Literature website). (etcsl.orinst.ox.ac.uk). Oxford: Oriental Institute at Oxford University, 2003.

Ryholt, K., Barjamovic, G. *Libraries Before Alexandria: Ancient Near Eastern Traditions*. Oxford: Oxford University Press, 2019.

Finkel, I.L. *The Ark Before Noah*. New York: Doubleday, 2014.

George, A., *The Epic of Gilgamesh*. London: Penguin Books, 1999.

George, A., *The Epic of Gilgamesh: The Babylonian Epic Poem and Other Texts in Akkadian and Sumerian*. London: Penguin, 2002.

Goff, B.L. *Symbols of Prehistoric Mesopotamia*. New Haven, CT: Yale University Press, 1963.

Grimal. P. *Penguin Dictionary of Classical Mythology*. London: Penguin, 1990.

Hachlili, R. *Ancient Jewish Art and Archaeology in the Diaspora*. Leiden: Brill, 1998.

Hilprecht, H.V. *The Earliest Version of the Babylonian Deluge Story and the Temple Library of Nippur*. Philadelphia: University of Pennsylvania Press, 1910.

Horowitz, W. *Mesopotamian Cosmic Geography*. University Park, PA: Eisenbrauns, 1998.

Jacobsen, T., *The Sumerian King List*. Chicago: University of Chicago Press, 1939.

Jones, A. *Ptolemy in Perspective: Use and Criticism of his work from Antiquity to the Nineteenth Century*. New York: Spinger, 2010.

Koch-Westenholz, U., *Mesopotamian Astrology* (*CNI Publications 19*). Copenhagen: Museum Tusculanum Press, 1995.

Koch, U. "The Astrological Commentary Šumma Sîn ina tāmartīšu Tablet 1," R. Gyselen La Science des Cieux (Res Orientalis 12), Science des cieux, 1999.

Lambert W.G. *Babylonian Creation Myths*. University Park, PA: Eisenbrauns, 2012.

Lambert W.G., "New Light on the Babylonian Flood," Journal of Sementic Studies 5, 1960.

Lambert, W.G., and Millard, A.R. *Atra-Hasis: The Babylonian Story of the Flood*, Oxford: Oxford University Press, 1969.

Leick, G. *A Dictionary of Ancient Near Eastern Mythology*. Abingdon, Oxfordshire: Routledge, 1991.

Lewis, J.P. A *Study of the Interpretation of Noah and the Flood in Jewish and Christian Literature*. Leiden: Brill, 1978.

Lloyd, S. *The Archaeology of Mesopotamia*. London: Thames and Hudson, 1978.

Mallowan, M.E.L. "Noah's Flood reconsidered", Iraq 26 No 2, 9 British Institute for the Study of Iraq, 1964.

Mallowan, M.E.L. *Early Mesopotamian & Iran*. New York, McGraw-Hill Book Co., 1965.

Mellaart, J. *Earliest Civilization of the Near East*. Thames & Hudson, 1965.

Miller, P.D. *The Religion of Ancient Israel*. Louisville: Westminster John KnoxPress, 2000.

Moorgat, A. *The Art of Ancient Mesopotamia*. New York: Phaidon, 1969.

Oats. J. *Babylon: Ancient Peoples and Places.* London: Thames and Hudson. 1986.

Oden, R. "Divine Aspirations in Atrahasis and in Genesis 1–11," 1981.

O'Flaherty, W., *The Rig Veda*. London: Penguin, 1981.

Oppenheim, A.L., "A Babylonian Diviner's Manual," Journal of Near Eastern Studies 33, 1974.

Oppenheim, A.L. *Ancient Mesopotamia* (revised edition.) Chicago,1977

Parrot, A. *The Flood and Noah's Ark. Studies in Biblical Archaeology I.* London: SCM Press, 1955.

Pennsylvania Sumerian Dictionary website (psd.museum.upenn.edu). Philadelphia: University of Pennsylvania, 2006.

Pingree, D. *Legacies in Astronomy and Celestial Omens.* Oxford: Oxford University Press, 1998.

Plutarch. *Moralia.* 16 vols. (vol. 13: 13.1 & 13.2, vol. 16: index), transl. by Frank Cole Babbitt (vol. 1-5) et al., series: "Loeb Classical Library" (LCL, vols. 197, 499). Cambridge (MA): Harvard UP et al., 1927–2004.

Raikes, R.L. "The Physical Evidence for Noah's Flood," Iraq 28

Ridpath, I. *Star Tales.* Cambridge: Lutterworth Press, 2018.

Selin, H. *Astronomy Across Cultures: The History of Non-Western Astronomy.* New York: Springer, 2012.

Smith, G., "The Chaldean Account of the Deluge," Transactions of the Society of Biblical Archaeology 2, 1873.

Smith, M.S. *The Early History of God: Yahweh and the Other Deities in Ancient Israel (Second Edition).* Grand Rapids, MI: Eerdmans, 2002.

Sukenik, E.L. *The Ancient Synagogue of Beth Alpha.* Piscataway, NJ: Gorgias Press, 1932.

Sun, K., *Our Place in the Universe: Understanding Fundamental Astronomy from Ancient Discoveries (Second Edition).* New York: Springer, 2017.

Roaf, M. *Cultural Atlas of Mesopotamia & the Ancient Near East.* Boston: Godine, 1977.

Rochberg, F. *In the Path of the Moon Babylonian Celestial Divination and Its Legacy.* Leiden: Brill, 2010.

Rochberg, F. *Heavenly Writing Divination and Horoscopy and Astronomy in Mesopotamian Culture.* Cambridge: Cambridge University Press, 2004.

Rogers, J.H. "Origins of the Ancient Constellations: I. The Mesopotamian Traditions." Journal of the British Astronomical Assoc. 108.1 (1998): 9–28. Astronomical Data Service.

Tigay, J. *The Evolution of the Gilgamesh Epic,* Mundelein, IL: Bolchazy-Carducci Publishers,1982.

Walker, C.B.F. *Astronomy Before the Telescope.* London: British Museum Press, 1996.

Wilson, I. *Before the Flood: Understanding the Biblical Flood Story as Recalling a Real-Life Event.* London: Orion 2001.

Wasserman, N. *The Flood: The Akkadian Sources Posted at the Zurich Open Repository and Archive.* Zurich: University of Zurich, 2020.

Watanabee, C.E. *Animal Symbolism in Mesopotamia.* Vienna: Institute fur Orientalisk der Universitat Wien, 2002.

White, G. *Babylonian Star-Lore.* London: Solaria Publications, 2008.

White, G. *Queen of the Night.* London: Solaria Publications 2014

Winter, I. *On Art in the Ancient Near East.* Leiden: Brill, 2010.

Reference to the online collections from the following museums were also made: British Museum, The Louvre, Metropolitan Museum, University of Pennsylvania.

FAQs

How accurate is the information in Heavenly Flood?

Heavenly Flood is based on the most recent research and scholarship on the ancient Near East. The book presents information in a clear and transparent way, and S.H. Scholar actively encourages his readers to experience the processes that the ancient mind underwent in making sense of the cosmos.

How do we know the positions of Mesopotamian constellations are accurate?

Various sources are used by researchers in determining how the ancient Mesopotamians saw the night sky. For an in-depth look at how the Mesopotamian star chart used in Heavenly Flood was created, S.H. Scholar recommends reading *Babylonian Star-Lore* by Gavin White.

How do we know the precessional movements of Mesopotamian constellations are accurate?

There are many accurate astronomy software programs available that will allow you to recreate the night sky from any location and any time period. You are encouraged to do this yourself. Simply locate the positions of ancient constellations using the Mul.Apin Text in Appendix 6. (p. 86) of Heavenly Flood, set your location to southern Iraq and compare their positions over various time periods.

Could the development of the Great Flood tale and precessional movements of Mesopotamian constellations just be a coincidence?

S.H. Scholar doesn't want to tell you what to believe. He just wants you to experience how the ancient mind may have seen and expressed the world around it. Once you have achieved this, you can make up your own mind.

How could a such a fantastic secret remain unknown for so long?

The ancient world often expressed secret information through allegory with its true meaning only being known to a select few. In a time when much of the population were illiterate and uneducated, the use of allegory was an especially effective way of keeping ideas secret over long periods of time. The advent of Christianity and its influence over the cultural development of the Near East eroded the propagation of ancient secrets in esoteric circles, eventually causing it to be lost to humanity, although it is likely some fragments managed to survive in various forms until fairly recently.

Acknowledgments

The conception of this book can be traced back to one dull winter evening in 2018, after having given my brother a personal tour of the British Museum. His resulting enthusiasm and insistence that I "should write a book about my insights into the ancient world" made me realize that there might be an audience willing to hear what I had to say. Therefore, I would like to acknowledge my brother on that fateful evening and his role in the birth of this book.

Expressions of gratitude are also due to Gavin White, author of *Babylonian Star-Lore* (Solaria Publications) with whose kind permission his Babylonian and Ancient Greek star charts have been included in this book. As far as I am aware, his Mesopotamian star chart is one of the first attempts at visually depicting Babylonian constellations and their position in relation to one another. This remarkable achievement has the effect of bringing us one step closer to understanding the ancient mind in a way that is more alive and visceral then the mere academic translations of the texts that the Babylonian star chart is based upon.

Made in the USA
Coppell, TX
24 October 2024